PROCRASTINATION

Easy Guide with Daily Habits to Build Self-Discipline, Mental Toughness, and Willpower. Cure Laziness and stop Self-Sabotage. Improve Time Management, Productivity and Gain your Goals

engaging in the rendering of legal, financial, medical, or professional advice. The content within this book has been derived from various sources. Please consult a licensed professional before attempting any techniques outlined in this book.

By reading this document, the reader agrees that under no circumstances is the author responsible for any losses, direct or indirect, which are incurred as a result of the use of the information contained within this document, including, but not limited to, errors, omissions, or inaccuracies.

TABLE OF CONTENTS

INTRODUCTION

A Guide to Overcoming the Procrastination

Procrastination means, in simple terms, putting off the things we know we should do. Everyone procrastinates at one time or another in their life, and it's natural. But it becomes a problem if we are unable to complete the tasks that need to be completed and we have expired invoices and tax returns, to deal with a lot of material on the morning of the exam day, to definitively clean the houses or to plan projects in the regular days not finished.

If the delay is extraordinarily chronic, and you are unable to do anything, you will probably need therapy. There may be psychological problems that need to be addressed or physiological problems related to the prefrontal cortex that need to be addressed.

But if you don't think you need a doctor, just a little more motivation, you're in the right place. Here are some steps to help you postpone the deferral. A caveat: none of these techniques will turn you into a complete non-procrastinator overnight, but will help you reduce procrastination and gradually gain self-control to keep the procrastinator in check when appropriately used effectively.

If anything, you must first determine and admit that you are hesitating. It is quite simple. If there is a nagging voice in the back of your head that pushes you to work on something, even if you "relax" or take some "free time," you will probably procrastinate. Or, if you are always late for the first and only draft of your order on the morning of the deadline, this may also give you an indication. If you are afraid of a big task you have to do, and it hangs over your head, and you are always worried, this is also a suggestion.

Why are you hesitating?

Next, you need to find out WHY you are hesitating. There are many different creative reasons that procrastinators find simply to put off this task.

1. There is enough time (self-deception and lack of motivation. Maybe because the job is inconvenient or uncomfortable)

2. It's not essential (self-deception again. Some tasks just need to be done, regardless of whether you think it's necessary or not)

3. I'm too tired (and you will be every time you take it off)

4. I take a half-hour break and then I do it (simple and uncomplicated procrastination. Again, the task is uncomfortable or uncomfortable)

5. Nobody seems to be in a hurry (rationalizing to escape a demanding job)

6. I'm not in the mood (and you probably won't be until it's too late, and then you'll start to torment yourself because you can't have overcome it when you've had the time))

7. I work better under pressure (self-deception. You don't work under pressure; you work simply because you have no choice. And if you had worked if the force had been lower, the results would probably have been better)

8. I want it to be perfect. I'll do it when I'm sure it's classic / I'm waiting for the ideal moment (inconsistent perfectionism)

Types of procrastination

All of this can be reduced to two basic procrastination types:

1. Relaxed procrastination

This type is when you think the activity can wait for another (more fun) activity to complete. The procrastinator finds excuses here that there is enough time, I will do it after resting/playing/watching TV, when I'm in the mood, when I have to do it, etc. These people have reduced self-control and are looking for **instant gratification. It is quite common.**

2. Procrastination tense

This guy is worried he doesn't have the skills to do the job. They may also be misfit perfectionists who continue to perform a task and wait for everything to be "just perfect." They worry a lot about the task, but they never seem to do it.

Overcoming the procrastination

Now the last step. HOW can you fight this? The approach depends on the type of procrastination you are making.

Relaxed procrastinate: You can try the following methods to start the business at your fingertips.

1. You can write a list of reasons why this is fine, even if you don't do it now. Next to each of these reasons, it is possible to write a counter-argument about why this is important now. For example:

There is enough time - I have used this motif a thousand times to postpone my studies. And in the end, I never have enough time. I always run at the last minute. Why am I not trying to study for a change now? I can always meet up with friends later.

2. You can tell everyone that you will soon complete the activity. And then peer pressure and your ego will make sure to do it;)

3. You can get help from a slightly domineering friend to make sure you don't give up.

4. You can reward yourself for completing the activities. For example, you can promise to buy yourself a chocolate mousse if you do the job before the evening.

5. You can take root if you don't do the job. Or refuse to watch your favorite show when the activity is not running. It works when you have a certain degree of self-control and deny yourself that you will do a show or a television treatment until the activity is completed.

6. View the completed task. Don't imagine the

process, only the result. If you want to clean the house, imagine what a well-kept house would look like, how proud you are to have finished it, how you can proudly bring friends home for dinner and how you can relax in this environment, Think about all the details of how different it would be the total energy of the room, how the carpet would look new, how the air would cool down. This will help you get started.

Tense procrastination: Here, you can try slightly different techniques to combat procrastination and fear.

1. Remember that no one has achieved great results by knowing all the details in advance. Tell yourself that once you start, you will find that the necessary resources are still available. Remember that if you keep going, you will find out.

2. Seek help from someone who knows the business better. Ask for advice on how to proceed.

3. Divide the task into really small, simple, and easy tasks. Complete them one at a time and focus only on the small task ahead. Complete the simple tasks, even if it is not the correct starting order.

4. Remember that over a certain amount, nitpicking

only kills time and creates no added value. Make sure the deadly rivers have been repaired, and if something else should arise, you can take care of it later, but the task is now done. Congratulations on your work, reward yourself. Continue with the next activity and freak him out.

These are some of the methods you can use to eliminate delays in your life. Remember, every time we procrastinate, we waste precious life energy, lower our vibrations, and reduce our karma. It is not worth putting things off!

THINK
+
POSITIVE

CHAPTER 1
WHAT IS PROCRASTINATION?

Procrastination can be defined as postponing actions or activities to a later date.

- It can be said that delay is the process of delaying essential tasks until a later date. In most cases, non-essential activities are performed instead of the more critical ones.

Psychologists refer to such behavior as a mechanism for coping with the fear associated with starting and executing an activity or decision.

- Usually, the person's behavior is hesitant

- Counterproductive

- Unnecessary

- delay

- Problems related to deferral include fear, low self-esteem, and a self-injurious mentality.

- procrastinators generally have a lower than average conscience.

- The approach is primarily based on the "dreams and desires" of perfection, contrary to a realistic assessment of their duties and potential.

Delay is a habit, but the good news is that, like any other habit, it can be broken.

- If this habit is not verified, it can have severe consequences for our lives and for the life of those who love us.

- procrastination becomes dangerous if it is further deactivated since it affects the mental and physical health of the person.

The delay is like a big bomb that violently detonates our personal goals. The things we sincerely appreciate are destroyed, and after the explosion, there is only regret. We tremble inside the internal earthquake that makes us feel empty.

Mike also claims that his sister's procrastination and "distraction" took more than $ 150.0270 from his bank account for over seven years. Delay is the profit thief that Napoleon Hill has advised us to overcome the delay: "The principle of concentration is how the suspension is overcome. The same principle is the basis on which both self-confidence and self-reliance are based. Self-confidence. Self-confidence. Appreciation. is expected. "

- The most important part of the job is the beginning.

- We have to stop analyzing repeatedly.

- We waste a lot of time, money, and energy if we aim for perfection in every task.

- If we take small steps, we withdraw from the delay and move closer to our goals.

Here are some tips to help you get started and avoid deferment:

- Determine that the activity must be carried out: there are no alternatives.

- **Self-reflection** helps us to determine our personality and to know why we avoid a specific task. Is it just our self-destructive behavior or lack of knowledge if I know and do the job?

- **Use positive instead of negative words** because words are colorful and influence us.

- Trust in our information, equipment, and deadline ensures that the task is completed on time.

- Through realistic expectations and prioritization of

tasks, we always have the objectives in view.

- Motivation and reward for yourself help us perform tasks efficiently.

Why People Procrastinate?

Everyone procrastinates. It is a human quality that everyone has experienced, but everyone wants them to do less. The reasons why people procrastinate can vary drastically, but multiple sources generally cause hesitation.

1. The fear of failure.

Many people don't start a project because they are afraid of failure. My favorite quote on this particular topic is: "A thousand-mile journey begins with the first step." If you never start, you will never know if you would have succeeded, and you will regret it for the rest of your life. Don't be afraid of failure. Bankruptcy is the most prominent teacher.

2. The fear of success.

A rare but still apparent reason for a change is the fear of success. In short, I would be amazed if you found out that this is your reason for hesitation. It is a deep fear that most people cannot recognize. If you have the slightest idea of putting it off for fear of success, you need to look carefully because you are afraid of success. You are probably only fearful of changes, and if the project is successful, changes in your life will ensue.

3. Not very motivated by the topic or possible result.

By far, the most common reason people procrastinate is not motivated enough to get started. This can be applied to so many things. For example, a student at school may not feel motivated to get a good grade and attend God College. These payments are extraordinarily distant and insignificant. It is difficult to be motivated by such a distant reward. Another example is that you are not currently interested in a job. You will certainly not feel motivated if you think that the work is useless or uninteresting.

4. There is no time limit.

Deadlines are one of the main reasons people discover they have a deferral problem. A period forces you to stop hesitating and do your job. However, if you don't have a deadline, you can wait for exhaustion. Deadlines are the ruin of procrastination, and the lack of deadlines is one of the main reasons why people procrastinate.

The Main Reason Why People Procrastinate

Many people are late when something needs to be done. In other words, many people procrastinate. If we procrastinate, they will delay the execution of specific tasks that may be important. You might think it's time to do something later, but what usually happens is that the period ends. Those who procrastinate to lose in the end. Why are we doing this?

People can delay projects for various reasons. Some do it because they don't have enough time or because they have other things to do that are more interesting. The reality is that it goes deeper. Fear of failure is one of the main reasons people procrastinate. People also procrastinate because of the fear of success.

Others procrastinate because they fear that the task they have to perform will prove to be wrong. They will do a lot of research and make them productive, but in reality, they procrastinate. You want things to be done right the first time. So procrastinate not to get confused.

These reasons may seem different, but they are all the same. The real reason it is easier to put off something than to do something that needs to be done is fear. This fear could be deeply rooted in the subconscious. So people don't procrastinate so much because they run out of time, but because they are afraid. In this case, the fear must be eliminated so that people do not procrastinate.

This may not work for everyone, but it may work for many others. To do this, you have to ask yourself why. Why are you afraid of success, of failure, or if you do something wrong the first time? Knowing that you are fearful of something is not enough; you have to understand why. This takes you deeper into yourself. Only then can you find and overcome the real reason for fear.

If people procrastinate, it can make them seem irresponsible. As a result, they are unable to live their life to the fullest. When people wait, it can lead to distrust of others because they may not be trustworthy for them. Finding the root cause of your fear is the first step in overcoming the delay. You will, therefore, be well on your way to enjoying life and getting rid of stress.

Main Reasons Why People Procrastination

If you take the time to do the things that need to be done and you have excessive delays, you can be a procrastinator. Are you always late and miss appointments? These are some characteristics. If you want to know more here, some reasons are why people procrastinate.

To make you aware of what the deferral is and to improve your habits, here are some suggestions. Once you understand what procrastination is, you may be able to make corrections to get a more reliable picture and reduce the stress caused by procrastination.

If the things you need to do are not organized, the responsibilities remain pending. At some point, they pile up. Sometimes it is difficult to get the energy going, which leads to an incomplete or late end.

If you have a schedule and are discussing a meeting or items to consider and you are not busy in a certain period or timeline, this is a sign. The delay in the upcoming task is a sign.

If you are in a situation that you cannot deal with, you may tend to avoid or postpone it because you are not sure what you can do. Doing things at the last minute when you have time to finish is a sign that you are hesitating. Bad work habits are developing, and it is a sign that you only want to focus on another direction.

If you are undecided, postpone another activity. This is another sign. Sometimes when things overwhelm you, you prolong the inevitable. Take your time; make a list. Stick to the plan to avoid reasons why people procrastinate, including you.

CHAPTER 2
FEAR OF FAILURE

Overcome Your Fear of Failure

The fears of disappointment is boundless; for justifiable reasons. Numerous individuals need achievement, yet just those individuals can defeat their apprehensions and accomplish the objectives they set themselves. Others, who are overpowered with fear and fail to address it, keep themselves from understanding their latent capacity.

The most exceedingly terrible thing about the dread of disappointment is that you can't satisfactorily take analysis or criticism. Instead, you tend to magnify the mistakes you've made in your life so much that it makes it difficult for you to free yourself from past mistakes.

The fact is, there are times when the fear of failure is so high that you tend to limit yourself to the point of not even feeling anything for fear of failure.

Why do you think you have to abandon the fear of failure? Well, if you don't let yourself go, you won't be able to achieve your desired goals in life. The fact is that the fear of failure creates a negative mentality that limits your options: it is as if you were not able to get what you want in life if you can just have the courage to go out and do it! But, hey, that's not all because of how your mind is programmed when you see that the brain is like a computer! OK, but you can change the harmful program you have, just as you can change the program with a computer.

The fact is, once you are brave enough to do something about this fear programmed into your mentality, you can give yourself the freedom to do what you want to do in life and achieve it. Here are some straightforward strategies that you can begin utilizing.

You must resist your fear. Seeing that the fear of failure subsides because you are so preoccupied with the fear that you don't even bother trying something you want to do: leave your goals out the window!

For this reason, be sure to take affirmative action for your life goal every day.

Remember, just say that if you don't achieve a particular goal, you have an understanding of the things you need and the qualities you need to have in the future to be successful and not be afraid for another goal; If you can, hey! It's even better!

What you need to remember is never to associate your failure with yourself because you can always get up and try other methods to achieve your goals. You can try doing things differently, because the means you use may be why you haven't tried to get what you want.

Consider the following questions as they can provide answers to your questions to help you overcome your fear of failure:

- Where did I make the mistakes?

- Could I have prevented the error in some way?

Where can I improve my work?

Remember that all mistakes must always be seen as a learning experience. This way, you have more chances to learn and do better next time. Think about it, and if you haven't made any kind of mistake, you wouldn't have the resources you need to change for the better. Good luck

The Seven Faces Of The Fear Of Failure

Seven Faces of The Fear of Failure

1.The fear of disappointment is across the board;

for justifiable reasons. Numerous individuals need achievement, yet just those individuals can conquer their feelings of dread and accomplish the objectives they set themselves. Others, who are overpowered with fear and fail to address it, keep themselves from understanding their latent capacity.

The most exceedingly awful thing about the fear of disappointment is that you can't satisfactorily take analysis or criticism. Correct this thought by reformulating your ideas or changing your beliefs. A revised view for an entrepreneur could be: "I will give 100 percent for the success of my company. If this fails, I will take what I have learned and change the business or start another with a greater chance of success". Most executives have had a severe failure on their way and use it to learn how to be more successful.

2. Procrastination. That face is more obvious. If you are afraid of failing and think you can fail, postpone the job, so you don't have to fail. An easy way to solve this problem is to define and take a small action. The success of the campaign will increase joy and confidence. Take one small step at a time until you have the courage and guide to move forward.

3. Anger. Instead of facing fear directly, express it as anger so that no one sees fear (maybe you too). We guys are good at this; We are not afraid of anything, are we? Anger in this situation is a protective response when we are so scared. My advice: overcome it and find the courage to face fear directly. Expressing anger, hiding fear usually creates a host of new problems.

4. Cry. Crying is a normal reaction to any type of fear, including the fear of failure. Most children do it openly, but for adults, it is usually best to do it privately. It is not for everyone and like anger, a camouflage for the primary feeling of fear. Crying can be cathartic, but after a good cry, you have to face fear directly.

5. Rationalization. This often happens in business development (e.g., The manager or sales representative who says after losing a big deal: "I didn't have much chance anyway"). Stop deceiving yourself! Stop making excuses. You will win a few and lose a few; however, the best way to win a large business is to play large, investigate everything, and figure out how to win and lose. This is what world-class athletes and top businessmen do.

6. Withdrawal. If the fear is so great that you are immobilized and withdraw, you may not be ready for the challenge. Either let him go or find someone to work with to find the courage and develop the skills necessary to increase your confidence and your chances of success.

7. Avoidance. You don't put yourself in situations where you think you can fail. This is a sure way of living your underachiever life. Work to rearrange your thoughts to win by trying 100 percent to get what you avoid (focus on the process, not the outcome).

We all try to protect ourselves from bankruptcies. Ironically, this makes us disappointing, one of the things we fear. All very successful people have failed, usually, more than the others, because they take more risks and, therefore, both fail and are more successful than the others. All fears can be addressed. Defend your size; strive to find ways to deal with fear.

The Antidote to The Fear of Failure

Fear of failure is one of the biggest fears in the world today. Sometimes people don't do what they should because they are afraid of failure. Fear of failure is equated with a fear of rejection and fear of criticism.

If you want to be fruitful, you have to diminish your fear of disappointment. Robert Edison has failed so many times before finding the light bulb. One thing that has kept him busy in his experiment is that he has never seen his mistakes as failures but as a consequence.

So many people, out of fear of failure, haven't realized 1/10 of what they can get.

To overcome this monster called **"Fear of failure,"** take these bold steps, and your fear of failure will be a thing of the past.

STEP 1: perform a bold action.

Do something you were afraid of. Not only do they act, but they also take bold and determined actions. You can change circumstances or situations. The fear of failure can only be overcome by something. Act now and do something.

STEP 2: Never give up.

Endurance is one of the main characteristics of successful people. Try different approaches or strategies until you reach the desired result.

STEP 3: never customize an error:

Nobody is a failure, and no failure is a characteristic of an individual. It's about results and results. Not having achieved the desired result does not make you a failure.

STEP 4: use different approaches.

If you always do something the same way, you will get the same result as a result.

If you don't get the desired result, try a different approach.

STEP 5: don't blame yourself.

Each error shows how a result or result cannot be achieved. So why kill yourself? Learn something from your mistake and correct it the next time you find that your previous action cannot lead you to your goal.

STEP 6: Learn from your failure.

Bankruptcy is, therefore, an opportunity to learn. If you fail, try as much as possible to choose something from the failed company. Try to identify the error, why it happened, how you could have prevented it, and how you can do better next time. Experience is the best teacher, so learn from it.

Overcome Your Fear of Failure

Fear of failure

Fear is what fills us with worry, fear, and stress. Fear of failure can be what makes you fail. We have to find out the basic problem before we can overcome the fear of failure. There are three main reasons for this: experience, lack of trust, and concern for other people.

Past experiences often shape our fears in the future. We cannot allow our fears to paralyze and frighten us. We should let it be a learning experience and improve further. We need to be aware that people who are successful today have failed at some point. Without this failure, some of them wouldn't even be where they are today. We must use bankruptcy to our advantage rather than letting you stop giving you extra momentum and motivating you to do better.

The next most common cause of this is a lack of trust that can destroy you on your own. Confident people are not afraid of failure because they know that whatever happens, they will succeed, even if they encounter bumps. No more bumps on the road keep successful people from being successful, as safer people have a more positive outlook on life most of the time. You are not worried and / or do not let circumstances or other people prevent you from reaching your goal. This brings me to the next topic, where we compare ourselves with other people and think about what they think.

We shouldn't be worried or confronted with other people. This means nothing but overloading us unnecessarily. We often worry about meeting others' standards rather than trying to meet our standards. We should create our meaning for success instead of trying to do something else for success. People will think and say what they want. All that matters is when you are happy and / or satisfied with what you are doing. Create your way and set your standards for what you like best, regardless of what others think, hear, or say about it.

In conclusion, we must use the failure of the past to our advantage, learn to build our trust, stop worrying about what others think or say, and try to meet expectations there instead of living ourselves. Once we have learned this and deal with the basic problem, we will move on to a better path and be able to let go of this fear of failure.

be
joyful
be joyful
May you
be
kind
be loving
be
May
loving
kind
be
kind
be
loving
bed
peaceful
May you
be
May I be
May you may
May you
kind
May be
be
connected
be
May
secure
secure
peaceful
be
be
be
secure
loving
connected
Maybe May
all
May you be
kind
connected
secure
be May
secure

CHAPTER 3
FEAR OF SUCCESS

Fear of Success: Overcome It for A Better Life

Fear of success is often the hidden factor that blocks your attempts to improve in one way or another. I will focus on weight loss in this section, but the principles apply to any goal you want to achieve.

Many people tend to combine the fear of success with the fear of failure, which I think is wrong.

Fear of failure is a deliberate fear that prevents you from trying because you fear the consequences of failure and failure itself.

While the fear of success is an unconscious fear of the changes that will be successful, this type of fear is much more difficult to identify and, until you do, you may find that you have not made it.

How do you identify and overcome the fear of success?

Identify

Let's tackle the identification first (horse in front of the car and so on!). The only important question you need to ask yourself is, "what if I can?" Write complete answers to your goals and how they affect all areas of your life.

This requires rational thinking focused on the reality of the situation. In other words, what is the most likely outcome of success, and what will change in your life?

It may take some time before you get real answers that go beyond your original thoughts. But this will be a good time because once you have these answers, it will be much easier to move on.

Any consequences of written success? Most likely, there will be positive and negative aspects.

Overcome

Look at all the negatives and see if they are rational or irrational beliefs. An irrational belief usually arises from a negative self-assessment. This can be reversed with a positive soliloquy.

Once the irrational negatives are filtered, the rational negatives remain, e.g., H. the realistic results of success that are negative. For example, losing weight can make you feel more pressured to stay at that weight, and people can show more interest in you (which is good for some). Others may not like the "new you."

The only way to overcome these drawbacks is from the front. You must face them NOW and accept them as part of your success. No success is good without bad. The sooner you accept that there are negatives, the faster you can deal with them and overcome your fear of success.

After deliberately identifying rational negatives, it's time to focus on all the positive ones. For weight loss, this could be the new body you've always wanted, the painless joints, the healthiest heart, and so on.

The positives far outweigh the negatives, and that's what you need to strengthen yourself every day.

Soliloquies

A common technique is a positive interior dialogue in the mirror. I used it in the past for my sport and now for my business. I admit that at first, it seems strange to speak to you out loud in the mirror.

Take some time and space when you do it, and it will be a more natural process. Just as negative conversation can lead to negative results, continuous strengthening of positive conversation will lead to positive results.

If you feel that you cannot overcome the fear of success through self-help, it is a good idea to see a cognitive-behavioral therapist. They have techniques to use your subconscious thoughts so you can start overcoming your fear.

In the end, however, it is up to you to make this commitment to succeed. Once the fear of success is overcome, you are more motivated than ever to train and eat well.

This combination of motivation and confidence leads you to achieve your weight loss goals and beyond.

Fear of Success - 8 Characteristics of The Fear Of Success

Some people are really afraid of being successful ... yes, it's true! Some people fear success.

And for the person who is afraid of success ... the fear is real. Others around the person may not understand it, often think that the person is illogical and ridiculous ... but the fear is very real and can be a serious obstacle to any real success in life.

How do you recognize the fear of success?

if you feel that something is holding you back

You know deep down that you are moving your way

if you think everything is out of control

if you can easily find distractions that prevent you from doing what you should do

if you have trouble concentrating your energy for a long time

if you lose motivation

when your trust ceases

Any combination of the above can indicate a fear of success!

Why is this happening? What is the fear of success?

They find the changes terrifying and want to maintain the status quo. In other words, you would rather leave things as they are. Changes often involve new experiences that can be viewed as frightening ... fear of the unknown

the belief that once success is achieved, it will be

expected to happen again. This is especially true of some students. I have met several students who are aware of their abilities and are convinced that they can do well, but they are also convinced that if they do well this time, they can be expected to do well every time. To avoid this, they make no effort. This can happen in all areas of life and at any age

As soon as success is achieved, expectations rise! People expect more from those who have been successful ... and the successful person tends to expect a lot from themselves and others. Some people cannot cope with the pressure of their expectations of themselves or the expectations of others

The success of attention can be overwhelming, especially if the person is very private and does not like to be the center of attention

Success is often associated with a lack of privacy in personal life, e.g., TV celebrities, sports celebrities, kings ... the lack of personal privacy can be too expensive to pay for success

Success, particularly in the commercial or professional sector, often leads to significant changes in the programs. Some people who are afraid of success fear that their family life will be disturbed, that they will have to work unreasonable hours and that their social life will stop

Success can attract negative feelings like envy, jealousy, anger from others. Friends and family members can suddenly treat the successful person. Differently, they can be jealous of the benefits of success and exclude the successful person. This would be extremely inconvenient for many people and should, therefore, be avoided at all costs

Success can change your personality and self-confidence. Success brings with it some feelings of success and success. Successful people tend to be more confident, friendly, and have more control over their lives. Some people fear that if they succeed, they will change

Fear of success is a real problem for some people … and it is a problem to be addressed.

Have you ever been afraid of success? I have had it several times in my life … and I know how it has affected my performance over the years.

A lack of self-confidence often accompanies the fear of success. The development and strengthening of personal trust make a significant contribution to reducing and eliminating the fear of success.

If your confidence is strong, trust your ability to cope with the changes that success brings.

Instructions to Manage the Fear of Progress and Satisfy Your Deepest Desire

Imagine learning to manage anxiety and being an essential model in your life.

The course of miracles states: "Reflections are seen in the light. In the dark, they are dark, and their meaning seems to reside only in changing interpretations, not in themselves".

It can be anything to learn how to fulfill your heart's dream, how to improve your golf handicap, start a new career, or create a blog.

Maybe you craved to revive lost love in a marriage, lose weight with yoga, develop a new financial mindset, or improve your life with more confidence.

Or maybe you quit smoking, or it's time to stop drinking alcohol or other addictions that take you hostage.

Overcoming the fear of success begins by reversing unfavorable explanations such as the ones above that only cause concern for failure and interest for an individual's rejection.

Life on your terms

Not being able to live life on your terms can be a disappointment that makes you short and helpless at the end of the reception.

Overcoming the fear of success means not losing confidence anymore, but only developing barriers that compete with personal improvement.

The Course in Miracles says: "Miracles are not competing and the number of them you can do is unlimited."

The implicit or unspoken message is: "What gave you the idea that you can't live life the way you want?"

Face the fear and disappear from the bank

He's like the man who finally built the football team, but the coach let him sit on the bench. What kind of sensations do you have?

What exactly does he need to overcome the fear of failure, get off the bench, and be the athlete, the person he wants to be?

This prevents him from expressing himself and letting the coach know that he is a fantastic person, and if he has the opportunity, he will demonstrate how unstoppable he is.

Sitting on the bench in life and not asserting yourself is like being in a single piece without playing the role. Are you going through life without being 100% committed?

Maybe it's because you think you can accomplish precisely what you've decided to do.

Are you starting to overcome the fear of success by not preparing yourself for failure and sabotaging your success by telling yourself that you cannot perform well?

Is it possible that you do not understand how to deal with fear because you activate an unfavorable and ineffective vocabulary to dominate your ideas?

Negative soliloquy removes your motivation to overcome the fear of success and is an internal barrier that needs to be removed.

Here are four ways to overcome the fear of success:

1.) Do you believe that your "pride in performing" motivates you to remove all "should," "thoughts," and "must" from your vocabulary?

2.) Think that you will provide 100% of everything you want to get. If you stop giving reasons for blaming yourself, you won't have the power to reach your goals and increase your self-esteem.

3.) Stay informed that accepting obstacles can be a kind of hypnosis for success. Go ahead in your interaction by eliminating all unfavorable soliloquies.

4.) Regularly "seeing" yourself in a development method. Feel and think that you are a dynamic, ecstatic, and productive person. Remember, your beliefs influence the order in which you act and feel.

Positive outlook

Remember that unfavorable soliloquy and bad attitudes prevent you from overcoming the fear of success, just as they can raise the fear of failure and the fear of rejecting an individual.

Just go out and do what it takes, research, investigate, perhaps hypnotize for success or whatever seems right, then take action to get exactly what you need to do in life come from the bank and be the person you want to be.

CHAPTER 4
PERFECTIONISM

Driving Perfectionism Out of Town

It's always useful to recall that when hairsplitting drives, disgrace rides the weapon.

PERFECTIONISM is at the root of many ills of unconsciousness that allow us to grow large trees of unconfirmed shame. I would like to try to illustrate.

When we protest against feedback that may or may not partially or partially reflect the truth, we feel that the feedback is well-intentioned, but there is something uncomfortable about it. It is a feeling of shame. Like "I should be on top. I shouldn't be fighting with it ... but I'm fighting with it. It drives me crazy."

Or, if we adhere to such high standards - which we usually have achieved - but can no longer - our perfectionism has turned against us, and our shame is now widespread. This is because our purpose has been shaken in some way. I'm talking about our primary goal in life - an existential purpose that we all have: life must be meaningful. Shame pushes this purpose into us.

Perfectionism is an often unconscious life in a lie. It is never useful in a sustainable way, even if it helps to obtain surprising results. So when we find that these results mean much less than we wanted, we are entirely disillusioned.

It is a pity this terrible reality, which can only be faced if we face it with vulnerability. Shame can no longer resist because it is vulnerable; it must be transformed into acceptance justified by truth. Acceptance is always liberating and frees us from joy.

The perfect answer to drive perfectionism out of the city is twofold: awareness of shame and our intention beyond that through vulnerability.

If we like to investigate our cause, we will soon discover that our expectations are set in something unrealistic. Such perfection is a sin. As Brown suggests, the intimate assistant of achievement is unfortunate. What else would take us to a person's silly place? But if we accept the place where life has led us, we are more able to look at life from a neutral perspective.

Driving perfection out of town means shaming the

weapon through deliberate vulnerability. The more we accept our breaking imperfections, the less we feel ashamed and the better our experience of reality.

While perfection holds the reins in hand, life with the rifle is miserable.

When shame rides the rifle for perfectionism, vulnerability rides the gun with acceptance. One is slavery; the other freedom.

The path through the break to completeness is self-acceptance of grace through vulnerability. But perfectionism takes us away from the joy and not towards pleasure.

Joy can only be experienced if we accept the reality of our reality.

Does Perfectionism Hold You Back?

Perfectionism may seem like a desirable trait, but it can often prove to be an obstacle rather than an advantage. If you consider that nobody is perfect, perfectionists adapt to senselessness and disappointment.

Perfectionism is not just another name for laziness,

even if the results of the defects of the two characters are very similar (it can be challenging to do a lot in both cases). However, there are significant differences between perfectionism and laziness. Lazy people don't do things because they don't want to do them, or there is always a distraction that is much more tempting than the obligation that should be taken care of. Perfectionists, on the other hand, come to the same result of inactivity for another reason. They believe that doing something is not worth it if it is not done correctly. This is not to say that the same person cannot have laziness and perfectionism at the same time or at different times.

Since it is difficult or even impossible to perform many tasks correctly, the standard of perfection can weaken terribly. Of course, there is a wide range of perfectionism, and most perfectionists, at least in some things, trace the line to do something. Shockingly, fussbudgets frequently spare their most ridiculous measures to stop profitability when it makes a difference. It resembles having a temporarily uncooperative mind, just that he can lift his terrible head anyplace else. What makes compulsiveness so unfortunate is that it is driven by low confidence, questions, and sorrow. Rather than considering the inability to be a learning experience and an unavoidable piece of being human, fussbudgets decipher their missteps as an indication of their dishonor.

Perfectionism is often caused by stressful relationships or stressful environments in the early years. For example, the most demanding parents could make their children vulnerable to perfectionism, letting their children believe that they should earn love through success rather than receive them unconditionally. The other extreme can be as bad as distant parents can make children feel unwanted and unworthy. Genetics also play a role in making someone a perfectionist, and the "nature versus cure" debate is unclear as to how much everyone impacts.

Perfectionists can pay a high price for their actions or their absence. Your fears and fears become self-fulfilling prophecies that can lead to worse and worse feelings and relationships. They disappoint themselves and those with whom they are connected.

However, there are ways to control perfectionism, both internally and externally. One way is to move away from excessively stressful relationships and environments. Of course, this cannot and should not always be so. There is a big difference between eliminating harmful stressors and merely hiding from the everyday stress that we all face.

The best way to overcome it is to look inside and realize that "err is human." Indeed, some of the most significant discoveries and learning experiences come from mistakes. All everyone can expect is to do their best. In this department, it can be useful to share your thoughts with friends, relatives, or specialists.

Perfectionism: Does It Keep You Messy?

Perfectionism is defined in the American Heritage Dictionary as a tendency to be dissatisfied with something that is not perfect, or that does not meet extremely high standards. Perfectionism is self-destructive behavior often masked by virtue. Many non-perfectionists often wish to be more like those who see them with "perfect" lives.

The desire to do high-quality work is perfectly acceptable. The limit is exceeded when perfectionism is a stubborn argument that negatively affects one person's life and the lives of others.

Perfectionism is self-injurious behavior that causes

fear and delay. Perfectionism can paralyze in some cases. Perfectionists often think they can start a project or business only if they can do it correctly. As long as they don't have the right tools and knowledge, they can't begin to. Often, when they start, they cannot complete projects because they constantly perfect their work to make sure it is perfect.

In an office environment, the perfectionist can have a desk covered with piles of paper. He can't do anything with batteries because he hasn't found the perfect system for storing documents or carrying out newspaper-related activities. So the batteries remain, and day after day, the perfectionist struggles for his imperfect office conditions.

Perfectionism weakens the entrepreneur. Imagine the opportunities that arise when the entrepreneur struggles with simple decisions that affect essential business functions. Find the perfect text for every letter or email, continually refine business records, and not be satisfied with anything. This is the life of the perfectionist.

Perfectionists often maintain their high standards, not just for themselves. They expect above average results from anyone who comes in contact. If they don't get these results, they can be offensive and sudden. Working with a perfectionist can be a difficult task.

There is hope for those of you who identify with what you have read here! If you know someone who is struggling with this problem, pass it on.

Talking to yourself is your worst enemy. Hear what your inner critic says about you. Contradict these claims with your statements. For example, if your inner critic tells you can't do anything well, a question that statement by thinking about things you've done well. What evidence does your inner critic need to support the comments he makes about you? Most of the time, the reports are wrong and utterly wrong.

Recognize that your value as a person does not derive from your performance in the different roles you play in everyday life. Keep in mind that if something goes wrong in your life or you make a mistake, it doesn't mean that you're an idiot or that you can't do anything right (or whatever your inner critic tells you). This may mean that you need training or improvement in this area of your life. If the feedback comes from outside sources, the problem may not be yours. Maybe the person giving the feedback is having a bad day.

Realize that perfection is an unattainable goal. Realign your goal to achieve excellence or mastery. You will find many more satisfactions.

Make mistakes on purpose. Since errors are hazardous for perfectionists, this is an experiment that can cause a lot of stress at first. Try "forgetting" to sign up for a meeting or course. Most likely, the manager will only remind you to log in. Get the feeling. You won't die, and nobody will think of you like an idiot. Mistakes are great opportunities to learn. If you don't make mistakes, you won't grow up.

I am...
a unique individual
safe from harm
the love I seek
my heart's desire
fully alive
the courage I seek
connected to all
not how I feel
completely enough

CHAPTER 5
A FEELING OF BEING OVERWHELMED

Trample: understand energetically, face it practically

Who has never felt overwhelmed by a situation before?

Know the real experience of oppression that occurs when you are stuck, insecure, and unable to decide what to do next.

We were all there and tried it.

However, have you ever thought about what the feeling of being overwhelmed from an energetic point of view means to you?

From an energetic point of view, it is time to feel overwhelmed, a delay to be precise. Overwhelming occurs when you are not yet up to date with what you said about the universe you want. It is the delay that occurs when the world has already delivered what you have asked for, and you are not yet ready to receive it.

Sounds like you?

If you are a spiritual entrepreneur, it is essential to understand what the feeling of being overwhelmed tells you energetically and how you deal with it in practice. Otherwise, the overwhelming will undermine your trust, make you doubt yourself, and put an end to your new beginning.

Don't let this happen to you! Here are five practical things you need to do to make up for what you said to the universe you wanted.

Five simple solutions that you can use to meet your needs

1. Take a walk.

Since the feeling of being overwhelmed is initially perceived as tense in the body, it only makes sense that the revitalization of the body helps move the energy that accumulates there. This is not an ideal opportunity to kick back and meditate. This is the time to move your body, pump your heart, and breathe deeply into your diaphragm.

Whether you are walking in your neighborhood or taking a relaxing walk in the mountains, you can get your whole body moving to dissolve the pent-up energy.

2. Flip a coin.

If you feel overwhelmed and can't choose between two options or approaches, flip a coin. Make a decision on one side of the coin and the second on the other. So turn around. Notice how you feel a split second immediately after the coin lands. Do you feel relieved, or your hopes have been disappointed? If you find that you are negotiating with "the best two out of three," you have made the right decision for you at this point. The delay that prevented you from getting what you want will dissolve immediately.

3. Do activities for the right brain.

Right brain activity is generally creative and innovative, while left-brain action is rational and linear. The great thing is that when the right side of the brain is excited, chemical changes are made in the body and brain, which are extraordinarily healing and stimulating.

Right brain activities include music, sex, art, massage, chromotherapy, aromatherapy, acupressure, polarity therapy, and much more. The main thing is to have fun and have fun!

4. Ask your subconscious a question. Put some paper and a pen on the bedside table before going to bed. Before falling asleep, ask your subconscious for an answer to your confusion. Capture your dreams or insights when you wake up.

5. Ask yourself what you would do if you took the opinions of others out of the equation.

It is often questioned what others think, what causes the delay between what the universe has produced, and your ability to receive what you desire. To counter this, remove the opinions of others from the equation. Now, what decision would you make?

Despite where you are in your business, chances are you have felt overwhelmed without a moment's delay or another. The kind of bullying that turns you off and causes paralysis. As a spiritual entrepreneur, it is important to understand what is going on energetically and how to deal with it in practice.

Are You Caught in A State of Abuse?

Do you find it overwhelming to fill you with a series of emotions at the same time? You don't go on, you feel stuck, and you're still on the daily treadmill just to do everything and pay those damned bills. You feel exhausted and empty, and, frankly, it's too difficult. You can experience physical ailments in many areas of your home and life.

You may be very depressed. You drag yourself to work, and everything is a great effort. You sit at your desk with a deep sigh. After about an hour, your mood will fade, and you will feel alive again. Spend the day feeling slightly tidy, but everything is so exhausting. Maybe you're so exhausted that you make mountains from moles. Bullying is a normal condition for you.

In short, you feel empty, exhausted, and dry, but the more you analyze it, the more overwhelming you feel. You are unhappy that all that stuff is going on and grumbling for the family. You also have an internal dialogue that tells you that you are ... also something, and would prefer to hide under a rock for the next month or so.

You can be a very sensitive person who absorbs energy from others. You feel a little strange like you're in a dream. The absorption of other energy is like a radio frequency, which is located between two channels and is reproduced on both. You lose focus and feel set to automatic all the time. If you can imagine two people standing next to you, one on each side and both speak to you at the same time It is difficult to hear what is being stated, and there is a kind of overload or chaos, so you say immediately, wait, stop, one by one. This feeling is intrusive and abuses our well-being. If the overload doesn't go away, sadness, anger, and frustration increase. Well, I'm here to tell you that people have lived in a constant state of abuse and still do, but it doesn't have to be that way.

Many people turn to addictions such as overeating, medications, drugs, or alcohol to numb these overwhelming feelings, hoping that their efforts will simply stop everything. This is a short term solution that doesn't work. Overwhelming is common.

So you are overwhelmed by overwhelming feelings that can seem like a dense, negative, or blocked energy, and that affects your functioning, your emotions, and your well-being. You need a way to get rid of this severity while restoring your energy field.

Some quick ways to solve this problem are a long walk in the bush and the only time to dive into the sea. Walk barefoot along the beach to heal energy, purify the aura, or perhaps hear a damn cry. Above all, it is important to maintain a sacred space and peace to stay away from others. Once your energies are clean, you need to keep it as often as you need, maybe once a month, maybe more. This will improve an incredible nature and give you the genuine feelings of serenity you are searching for.

If bullying is something that is experienced regularly, working with a bully coach is the most effective way to change old attitudes, replace old beliefs and habits that you no longer need, and move to a place of inner knowledge, clarity, and happiness.

<u>Three steps to overcome coaching:</u>

1. Identify and reveal thoughts and beliefs that overwhelm you

2. Activate the internal power source

3. Use simple tools and techniques for energy management

<u>**The benefits of coaching include:**</u>

Feelings of satisfaction

Renewed clarity

A lot of energy

Refreshed mood

Greater awareness

Goal-oriented focus

Positive attitude

Energized realization

CHAPTER 6
LAZINESS

Overcoming Laziness

Jules Renard, a well-known French writer, once said: "Laziness is nothing but the habit of resting before getting tired." Yes, we can laugh at this statement, but it doesn't ignore the truth in it. Laziness is an indicator of disinterest in an activity characterized by a feeling of emptiness. Doctors claim that laziness is both a physical and mental state caused by a lack of interest in activities.

Many of those who succumb to laziness sit around wondering what to do. Laziness usually arises when you have idle moments. The trick to overcoming laziness is never to have a lazy time. It is what you should remember to overcome laziness when you receive something and see that it is done. The following methods have been shown to achieve this:

• Name some activities you like best and do at least once if you feel lazy. Fun is a motivating factor for overcoming laziness.

- Leave boredom aside. If you're interested in your job, it's about rewarding yourself for performance and praising your strengths.

- The trick to achieving goals is to divide bloated pieces into small and feasible tasks. You can't achieve a goal if you do all the things at once. This leads to the feeling of being overwhelmed and consequently lazy as your mind can be conditioned by the fact that you cannot and simply cannot do the activity.

- Training and exercise are also tools for overcoming laziness. This will consume your repressed energy and think of happy thoughts as you burn calories. It also helps you get fit and have a sense of accomplishment.

- Realistic and achievable goals are the right way. Use sticky notes, calendars and organizers to remember your goals. Simple goals are easier to achieve than gigantic ones. Start with simple ones first.

- Moments of inactivity are a no-no. At least find something to do or start something valuable like home improvement or a list of things to do with the whole family and even friends.

Delay is the workshop of laziness. To overcome laziness, you need to get things done immediately or as quickly as possible. Start with the simpler ones, and you'll have a sense of accomplishment when you're done. This gives you additional motivation to start the more difficult ones later on.

• Novelty is the right way. Routines can be boring. Add other useful activities to your day, e.g., B. a brisk walk in the park or a coffee break with friends or colleagues. This way, you can reduce stress and make more friends. You can overcome laziness by engaging in goals.

Laziness is only a state of mind. Get over it with a little persistence and use your mental and physical abilities. Go! Now get over laziness.

Laziness Is an Enemy In You

Laziness is in him for a man and an enemy. It is a complex trait of a person who contradicts logic or reasoning. Laziness can be defined as slowness, slowness, inactivity, or slowness of a person, which hinders the growth and progress of one's life. Therefore, laziness keeps a person poor. Procrastination is another form of laziness that causes a person to prevent or postpone a project or work indefinitely. Laziness can also be equated with lust, which keeps a person inactive in bed so that they are more likely not to get out of bed and continue their routine activities. In short, laziness can be defined as a mental block of a person who remains static and neglects his duties.

The cause of laziness is due to the days of childhood. A child takes the laziness of his parents and is anchored in it. Therefore, a child's parents must be accused whose laziness and attitude infect a child. When seniors and children watch TV together for hours, they are addicted and neglect their developmental and other important activities in life. For example, an elder cannot finish his office job satisfactorily in his office while the child neglects his studies and performs poorly in exams. The procrastination or the tendency to postpone work or a project lead to an excessive delay, which leads to another form of laziness.

All religions have taken note of laziness and its disastrous effects on humanity. The Bible uses anecdotes to explain the bad effects of laziness on humanity. Buddhism wants to avoid laziness. Islam recommends hating laziness.

It is, therefore, our duty to refrain from laziness in the interest of our good and humanity. But it is not an easy task. First of all, we should motivate ourselves. So we should make joint efforts in the right direction. Some tips on how to get rid of laziness will not be out of place.

To close the door on laziness, we should start with the man's father, the boy. Parents must set an example for their children when it comes to avoiding laziness by doing everything systematically and methodically without delay. We can avoid delays in large projects by dividing them into small segments and completing them one after the other in a set time. This also allows us to learn time management. People who want to get rid of their laziness can have specific goals, depending on their abilities and backgrounds, and pursue them with a single goal and concentration. Your laziness is gone once and for all.

The Myth of Laziness

Laziness is an excuse used by unconscious people (who do not know what to do with themselves) to make the most conscious people feel bad if they do not carry out insignificant tasks and tasks with them. You want to do the benefit of others.

Lay terms: laziness is a term used by people to try to criticize others who are too smart or too sure of wasting time doing things they would rather not do.

According to this logic, if you don't want to work in a booth and earn a salary - while you are insulted and marginalized by a sociopathic boss and by a sneaky and dramatically motivated staff - then by default, you are my friend! What a pity for you! ;)

"Can't you be careful at school and do your homework? You have to stop being so lazy and fasten your seat belts!"

"Haven't you found a real job yet? What are you, you idiot?"

"Why don't you work more hours? You must be lazy!"

Again, people are not lazy. They simply prefer not to engage in activities that bring little or no real accomplishment to them.

The truth is that laziness is largely a myth. Nobody is lazy by nature. Some people find it tiring to constantly force themselves to act and behave in a way that doesn't match what they are inside.

Do you know who the only real lazy people are ?! Those who scream and shout at people with alternative goals for laziness, but plan their entire lives with the "goal" of retiring at 65 and doing nothing for the rest of their days. This is lazy!)

Nobody is lazy

Do you like doing things you don't want to do?

Are people's opinions enough to make you insecure if you don't agree with what others are doing with their time?

Is your self-esteem tied to external authorization triggers, primarily to other people?

How many times do you perform actions, activities or habits just because it is easier to manage than when you have to listen to someone who makes you look ridiculous because you are "too lazy" not to do it?

There is a major contrast between somebody who plays Xbox, drinks Mountain Dew and sucks on government support while not trying to improve themselves or their situation and someone smart enough to recognize that most are traditional. Occupation is a serious compromise: you are self-employed and spend most of your time under the supervision of someone else who does eight hours a day of tasks that have nothing to do with each other.

The ironic thing is that the first example is considered more "normal." We are often taught to connect people with alternative ideas for life as high-risk individuals, often stupid in their attempts to make it out of a job.

The biggest risk, however, is not taking any risk.

The biggest risk in this life is that you spend your time finished doing boring and repetitive tasks that have nothing to do with your real passions and solicitations because you are too shy to exceed expectations and be truly involved in the objectives that inspire you.

The only risk is risk aversion

The only people who complain about the risks are those who are too afraid actually to take them.

Not all risks are created equal. Risk is a relative term and can mean many different things. Starting a business is a risk, and the level of this risk depends on the amount of initial capital that an individual must "risk" to invest. They know there is a possibility that they will not profit from their company, but it is a risk they take and accept.

Even those who feel superior to their unwavering ability to comply with the rules and regulations adopted by an arbitrary authority are themselves taking an enormous risk.

Instead of **"risking"** their illusory self-esteem by working towards a legitimate, passionate, and motivated goal, they put their identities aside to avoid this situation.

The opinions of others become the price. This, therefore, confirms their self-esteem more than their actions.

These people complain quickly and call others not to "adapt" to the rest of the herd. Still, they will be the last to take a personal risk, which does not include the possibility of rewarding someone whose deception causes them to do something to do what they would prefer not to do.

Time is your greatest asset in this life

Time - NOT MONEY - is your greatest asset.

Money can always be replenished.

Time cannot be.

Therefore, it is advisable to prioritize your time by filling it with activities, people, and places that fill you with a true sense of self-fulfillment and happiness. It is a waste of your precious life to force yourself to take part in actions, like a job that you have.

You're infinitely better going to ruin and doing something you love.

You have too much potential to waste an insignificant and insignificant job, which means nothing to you and does not contribute to achieving your true and passionate goals.

They have too much value to limit you to the standards of other people and organizations who only take care of filling your pockets and telling you what you need to listen to so that your dreams are put on hold indefinitely.

Don't let someone else set you free from your dreams with the promise of comfort and safety. Security is also an illusion, remember?

People with self-esteem and self-confidence don't need external permission to pursue their goals. The only people who have to resort to excuses, like calling someone lazy not to be socially conditioned, are those who are too afraid to start their lives. You have to hold your hands wherever you go because heaven forbids you from experiencing failure! Oh no, we don't want that, do we?!;)

You are not lazy just because you don't want to do boring, insignificant, boring tasks and you want to work like everyone else. Most likely, they are infinitely smarter and more aware of most people. So pat yourself on the back because you dare to recognize it and speak! Now fill your time with something you're excited about!

Simple Ways to Combat Laziness

Laziness can do things and keep you from reaching your goals. If you are suffering from lethargy, you may not be able to do your homework, stick to your exercise program, and even take care of your dreams and growth. This is because when laziness begins, you put off the things you should do next, and this can end in a cycle, which means you are doing fewer and fewer things.

If you were wondering how to stop being lazy, you should first know that fighting laziness is possible. The best thing about fighting laziness and idleness is that you don't have to make too much effort. Some changes may be all you need in your daily routine to finally stop relaxing and keep it away if you feel like sneaking in. Here are a few things that can assist you with staying away from apathy.

Start with an exciting little step: if you don't find the strength and motivation to do things, how about reducing this inner resistance through exciting action? Just running for five minutes, or even five minutes to wash dishes, can be all you need to do the daily work. If you worry a little bit about everything you need to do, it can work incredibly well, even if it only takes a few minutes.

Start the day by doing some key things: there may be so many things to do every day, but some are more important than others. Discover them and start the day doing the most important things, even if you only do a little. If you divide activities into smaller activities, it becomes easier to focus on them.

Get enough sleep, rest, and do some exercises. One of the main reasons why people feel lazy is that they cannot find enough rest and sleep. The truth is that if you have enough rest, exercise, and sleep, the next day, you will enjoy more energy, strength, and enthusiasm for doing things. Plan your day so that you have some time to rest, get enough sleep, and do some exercises and not feel lazy at all.

Renew your motivation with the advantages and disadvantages of laziness - One of the best ways to make sure you keep working on what you need to do is have a clear vision of the future. List the things you want to accomplish and imagine this life. So think about where you will be when laziness continues and where you will be when you fight it and continue working for your dreams. Having in mind the negative consequences of laziness can bring very positive changes in your life to get you moving.

CHAPTER 7
BOREDOM

Boredom: Reasons and Remedies

Are you feeling bored? Boredom is common among people of all ages. I often hear people say that they are bored or that life is so boring. If someone says that life is so boring, it means that he loses interest in life. This type of negative development must be taken seriously.

There can be many reasons for boredom. A person who feels bored knows the reason for their boredom. **However, the most common reasons for boredom are:**

1. Do nothing. The main reason for boredom is that you have nothing to do. An inactive person is quickly bored.

2. No meaning in life. If you have no purpose in life, no goal and no goal, get bored and say, "Life is so boring."

3. No friends. If you have no friends to hang out with and enjoy life, you will be bored. Life also becomes boring when no one shares and enjoys your happy moments.

4. The same routine work. Many people get bored doing the same job over and over again.

5. Don't appreciate it. If you do a good job, but nobody appreciates you, you can become depressed and bored.

6. Feel the emptiness from within. If you feel empty or empty from the inside, it can also lead to boredom.

If you feel bored, you don't want to do anything, and this increases your boredom. To overcome the feeling of boredom, most people temporarily watch TV, but this is fatal because they feel depressed and bored when they change.

There are some temporary solutions to overcome boredom problems, such as: taking a long walk, doing yoga or aerobics, talking to a friend, drawing cartoons, singing, dancing, etc.

However, for a permanent and positive solution to boredom, you need to do the following:

1. Don't sit idle. Do something that interests you.

In your spare time, read a book, write an article, or call a friend.

2. Be proud of your job, and enjoy your job instead of getting bored. Try to do your job better. If you don't like your job, you'd better quit.

3. Draw a detailed success plan of your life and focus on it. Set realistic goals and follow this step by step.

4. Also, celebrate your little successes in life. Use every opportunity to enjoy life.

5. Compatibility of work and family. Spend time with your spouse and children. Plan some leisure activities with your family.

6. Continue to dream and improve yourself.

7. When you feel empty in life, connect to God. Start praying and meditate.

8. If something disturbs you, go to the root cause of the matter and try to resolve it.

9. Remember that life is not boring. It is a gift from God that you can enjoy. Life becomes boring when you start living aimlessly. If you follow the meaning of your life, you will never be bored.

Are You Getting Bored?

"I'm bored" is a phrase that parents often hear, especially because the summer school holidays are longer than four weeks. Children who couldn't wait to drop out of school suddenly got bored with what they had been looking forward to for months.

But boredom is not only felt by children. Consider these statistics:

- A Gallup poll published in the Washington Post (10 August 2005) found that 55% of all US workers "were not involved in their work."

- Twenty-four percent of employees interviewed by Office Angels say that boredom has pushed them to rethink their careers and look for alternative jobs (The Guardian, January 20, 2003).

- A third of Brits say they are bored at work for most of the day (DDI Faking It survey, 2004).

- In a 1998 survey, nearly 45% of recruiting experts said that companies lost the best workers because they were bored with their work (Steinauer, 1999).

A definition

Dictionary.com defines boredom as: "the state of

boredom: boredom; boredom." Perhaps the synonyms (boredom, depression, tiredness) and opposites (excitement, distraction, fun) are so instructive.

Boredom is often described as tired, tired, or uncommitted. Some components of boredom are:

o tiredness

o dissatisfaction

o fear

o Irritability

If we or others experience boredom at work (the study says you don't get bored when you work with someone), it harms retention, job satisfaction, job quality, and overall productivity.

Solutions

Think of these solutions as an incomplete list: there are many other specific solutions, especially if you are considering boredom without work. However, if you do one of these stages, it can have a significant, perhaps lasting impact on boredom and the problems associated with it.

Also, consider the specific ideas mentioned

that you can use as a manager to help others implement this idea.

1. Search for meaning. If you know how important your work is to others (internal and external customers, your team, perhaps even the company as a whole), it is less likely that you will get lost or bored. As an individual, look for ways to understand how your work matters. As a manager, make sure that employees recognize a clear connection between their work and the goals of the team, department, and organization. Help people give their customers a face. Offer people a job they consider special. When people see how they positively affect others, boredom is greatly reduced, if not eliminated.

2. Be curious. Active minds are less bored. If we are actively curious, our minds will keep moving! As a leader, you can encourage curiosity and creativity by giving people leeway for their professional responsibilities and expectations. Give people time and resources to work on specific projects that are of interest to them and match their natural abilities.

3. Make it unforgettable. When tasks seem trivial, common, or routine, boredom can take hold. Find ways to make your job more memorable by adapting your routine or trying something new. Try your work in a new place or from a new perspective. As a manager, leave some flexibility in this area if possible. Encourage your team to set new records, to work with other people or to enrich their work or work environment.

4. Act. Boredom is often accompanied by tiredness or lethargy. The best cure for Blah is to act! Start with a new goal, step on an existing goal, or learn something new. If you do something, boredom will subside. When managers support people in setting meaningful and challenging goals, boredom also subsides. If your team's employees can do their job in less than a full hour, challenge them with an important addition for both those employees and your business goals. This could be an exciting project, an opportunity to learn, to lead a new colleague, as long as the person is excited to do it and doesn't feel like they are just adding more work.

5. Focus on others. Boredom rarely arises when you focus on someone who is not yourself. Think about the things you can do to improve the lives of others. In your personal life, this could serve as a volunteer or do something for a neighbor, friend, or family member. At work, offering help on a project can be so simple. As a leader, it can be so easy to encourage people to help others. Also, understand that if you help people see more meaning in their work, you will also help them divert attention from themselves.

Even if you don't get bored often personally, adding more of these solutions can improve your attitude and increase your productivity. Think of leadership ideas as ways you can help others regardless of their role and relationship.

Potential note: Boredom can have a huge impact on job satisfaction, energy, and productivity. Reduce boredom by proactively reducing causes - make work more meaningful, be curious, make work memorable, act, and focus on the needs of others.

Overcoming Boredom

Boredom affects both people at home and at work. You should always be careful and avoid it.

The following ideas and suggestions can help you avoid boredom at work.

For those used to working hard, job satisfaction and performance are important factors that make them happy. Boredom at work can kill all of this and plunge you into depression and also affect your productivity. We would like to present some ideas that can be implemented to overcome these boredom situations at work.

This is the best time to access the intranet and find out more about your company. You will learn all about the organization you work for, including its policies, visions, and goals.

If you understand the philosophy and culture of your company, you have the opportunity to identify yourself with your company and apply the same values in your working life. It also dissolves boredom at work.

The best way to keep boredom at bay is to interact with others in your office and renew your relationship. When you know others and find out where they are in your career, you can exchange mutual knowledge and experiences that can be useful for both.

If you don't find any challenges in your current job and do routine tasks, you will probably be bored. Once you recognize this, it's best if you apply for a job change or move to another department and start something new.

Changing some of the daily routines and doing things differently can make your office more varied. Discuss with your team how to promote extracurricular interactions and activities.

If boredom and monotony at work consume you, you must try to change your routine and do something more fun, and that makes you feel good. It can be to buy a new expensive watch or a bag or treat yourself to ice cream.

If you've learned the art of overcoming boredom at work and acting, then the sky is the limit. Nobody can stop you from reaching the height you are looking at.

3-Way Cure for Boredom

Here are three tips on how to cure boredom when

you're stuck and trying to do something:

Boredom Killer # 1. Leave the house. This is the oldest antidote to boredom in this book.

Sometimes I get bored at home. If your boredom started at home, you must be tired of fixing the same things. So the instinct is to go out!

Arriving at a friend's house or shopping center, try the park. Take the dog out if you have one. You damn well know he's been holding onto his shit since you got home - he will love you forever if you give it up! Do something so you can get away from the region of your home where you got bored.

Heal my tip for boredom # 2. Try not to return for at any rate 60 minutes!

If you somehow manage to escape your 'boredom' for an hour, then I guarantee you that this area is not so dull when you come back! Stay away at least for a long time. This is just enough to make the place where you got bored "fresh" again.

Cure for boredom # 3. Do something fun!

What do you like to think Thinking is a cure for boredom in itself? Going back to the topic, when you play a sport, you will find a friend who is ready for a game. It doesn't have to be really competitive, but if competitiveness is your motivation, do it! A quick game of soccer, basketball, football... these things can shoot boredom in the face!

The social aspect is vital. Being able just to see a face you haven't seen in a while, say two days or so, should be enough to get bored. A good friend can be a murderer for boredom.

There are other ways to keep boredom at bay than to leave the house. I will list the first three.

* The computer = game + internet: um ... you can't go wrong there. If you are not the "god of the Internet," you may have seen it all, but you can still find all sorts of exciting things that will help you cure boredom.

* Console games: Xbox 360, PS3, and Wii allow you to choose your boredom killer who can satisfy you for hours or even days or weeks.

* Watch the movie: I prefer the horror and action genre as a means of choice for boredom, but any type of film that stimulates your mind should be a suitable

antidote to boredom.

The thing is, you have to try every now and then to detach yourself from everyday life. It is the only sure way to cure boredom that is different from what you did to get bored against boredom!

CHAPTER 8
NEGATIVE SOLILOQUY

How to Stop The Negative Chatter?

I see a huge amount of negative conversations every day about how people feel about themselves and see the consequences. It is the continuous flow of destructive chatter and negative thoughts that prevent us from reaching our full potential - potential that is just waiting for you.

What should be considered here is that the musings we think decide an incredible result. I am a product of your environment. What you think, what you believe corresponds to what is manifested in your life.

Guess what your life experience is? The Grand Master: CHOICE.

You can choose the thoughts you think. It is easy to become cynical because we have been trained and continue to focus on our perceived limits and more. But what about the positive? How about if you really know you are an extraordinarily precious and naturally beautiful person who deserves to have all the best in the world?

Most people are generally very self-critical. And these habitual negative thoughts unfold in various ways in our lives. Negative thinking is a habit, and all practices can be changed. Habits require minimal mental process and no willpower: they are comfortable and automatic.

Implement these three keys to success to create the life you want:

-Take bigger targets in small steps.

Start with small steps to create new habits. For example, if you are trying to end the practice of talking negatively about yourself instead of stopping a cold turkey, you decide to talk about yourself positively once a day for a week, increasing week by week. The transition to positive soliloquy will, therefore, create success for you, and this success will motivate you to move forward until it automatically becomes a different life experience.

-Be Consistency

Consistency is critical because daily practice creates stronger neural connections, which then allow new positive behavior to become automatic - a habit.

Whenever you think of a negative thought, replace it with a positive one.

- Start a diary.

Writing down your thoughts not only helps reduce stress, but it also helps you objectively recognize where self-criticism and negative thinking go in your life. This information is essential to create a new paradigm.

You are what you think. If you consciously choose to stay away from negative thoughts, an entirely new world will open up to you. Remember what you feel about yourself, and your world will become your life experience. So if you think it's not worth it ... guess what? Your life experience will be less than you deserve. However, if you choose to think differently by focusing on what's right in your life, what should happen, and feeling more positively, you will live the life you love.

Three Tips to Getting Rid Of The Negative Soliloquy

Negative soliloquy negatively affects your success

and potential. When you use negative words and thoughts to talk about your actions and results, you literally weaken your self-esteem and lose the power of yourself. If you think you are negative and speak for yourself, how can you expect others to treat you differently? Here are three tips for getting rid of this bad habit of negative self-talk.

Tip 1: start the day more carefully

Start every day with the vision that everything is going well. Find out how to fix things, floating happily and smiling during the day. Remember that you can do it, which is natural and fun to be in that state.

If you learn to start the day on a positive note that you have created in your mind, you will find that this more positive attitude means that you don't have to be so hard on yourself during the day. The more you put yourself in this type of posture or mood, the less you will fall into harmful speech. You will laugh at your mistakes more easily than criticize yourself.

Tip 2: Create a mantra or confirmation of encouragement

You have endured many problems and failures in

your life and are still here, sometimes with success, sometimes not so much success, but in the end, you have endured it. Finding words that reflect this fact, your courage and your determination is the beginning of a better and more favorable personal dialogue. The positive inner dialogue begins with healthy self-esteem. Much self-esteem comes from the place where you can overcome failures and endure the rigors of life. Remember your innate ability to resist, no matter how small the success story is.

Tip 3: stop criticizing others

Generally, when you spend a lot of time criticizing others, you spend a lot of time in a negative attitude. Of course, it is easier to penetrate it into your inner dialogue. If you are very critical of others, you tend to be very critical of yourself. It works in both directions. Start noticing when you are significant and try to say something that is less critical or encouraging to the person or subject of your attention. One thing to remember is that many people like you do the best they can with what they have. It may not be the best solution, but it is probably the best solution you can find in these circumstances. This always helps to put an end to criticism and to seek thoughts, attitudes, and a better understanding of a particular situation.

Getting rid of negative inner dialogue means learning to look at life from a more positive perspective. Start small and look for little good things in your life, in yourself, and in the actions you take. If you direct your attention in this way, those bad words that overthrow you will be eliminated.

How to Stop The Negative Inner Dialogue?

Thousands of thoughts come to mind every day. We are aware of some ideas and not others. Even if you are familiar with the law of attraction and start thinking and acting to attract what you want, you may also have noticed that it is straightforward for the mind to do a little harmful speech each time it gets the opportunity.

Why do we have to fight negative chatter?

You have to understand that your brain and mind contained nothing negative at birth. In other words, nobody is born with negative thoughts that await development somewhere.

Negative thoughts are learned. Very soon, we learn

what we cannot and cannot do. We hear the word "no" about three times more often than the word "yes." We feel the stress and negativity of parents and people who influence us as children very early. In addition, we learn even more negativity in school and other places. When we grow up, we are well made, so to speak.

This is why we must basically fight negative inner dialogue if we are not yet familiar with the law of attraction.

Here is an example of what many people do. Let's say we decided we wanted to make $ 3,000 in 3 months. This money does not come from sources of income that you already have. Add $ 3,000 to travel around Europe.

Now you have learned to display the amount of $ 3,000 in your bank account on a check in hand. You can see how to process and count the money once per invoice. You also learned to visualize the entire journey in all its details.

Every now and then, a voice in you tells you how I get that $ 3,000? I don't see it now! Can I materialize this money? Can I really earn another $ 3,000 in three months? This is your negative soliloquy.

How can you stop negative chatter?

The best way to stop negative conversations once they appear in your head is to look at your thoughts by paying attention to what you think, just as you would watch your steps if you walked on rough terrain.

Whenever you are aware that a negative conversation is starting, just stop it and stop it. So try replacing it with a positive one. Use everything that comes to your mind only to end the negative chatter at that moment. If you do it more and more often, you can catch yourself in the act more often. The more often you replace your negative conversations with the positive ones, the faster you can achieve the desired life.

CHAPTER 9
INABILITY TO MAKE A DECISION? TIPS FOR BETTER DECISION MAKING

Making decisions can be one of the most painful things you need to do. Of course, not all decisions are created equal, and some decisions are easier than others. However, there may be some choices that leave you on the fence and, above all, make you feel stressed and crazy. They keep you from moving forward!

Decision making is essential for a thriving life. It improves the quality of life and is vital for your physical and mental health. The longer you postpone a decision, the longer it runs out in your mind and body. You have less peace of mind. The less you enjoy life. The less you want to face it. The more you feel victimized.

You might think that if you could only predict the outcome of your decisions, you would have no problem making this decision. Well, the point is, you can't always predict which is the best choice. That doesn't mean you should stay on that fence until you can predict something. The more you sit, the more awkward you feel, and the more likely you are to miss the opportunity that you would otherwise have liked.

So, what to do

Things to think about:

1. If you are unsure, you will become aware of what your indecision does to your mind and body. Would you like to keep living this way?

2. Find out your selection. There is always more than one choice. Is one feeling better than the other?

3. Research. Just because it is impossible to predict a result does not mean that an informed decision should not be made. Find out as much as possible from objective and subjective sources.

4. What would make you happy? It always depends on your luck. This means that you are making the right choice, and you are not deciding what the talented people in your life should do for you. In the event that you don't know what to do in your life, suddenly you feel like other experts and their advice seems very wise. Remember that you are your expert!

5. Make a decision, no matter what. The longer you sit on the fence, the less happy, grumpy, and uncomfortable you will be. Even an incomplete selection will give you relief.

Find Out How to Find Solutions And Make Decisions

Take a moment to think about the last time you had to find a solution and make a decision about a problem in your business or life. What method or process did you use? Were the solution and the decision reactionary? Or have you had a process not only to make a decision but also to find a long-term solution?

Individuals often practice making permanent decisions based on temporary circumstances. This type of thinking does not help you use your critical thinking skills to examine, clarify, and determine the outcome of a particular life situation. Troubleshooting is not just about finding a working solution, but a multi-step process that allows you to deal with the situation logically and practically.

Evaluate the situation

Assessing the situation can be the long part of the process. However, it is an important component for developing solutions and making decisions. With this method, you can not only view multiple options but also view options in different ways. You can view options as a process from a creative perspective, a data-only viewpoint, an emotional response, both yours and others', when the decision influences them. Some of these perspectives are known as the "six thinking hats" theory, which can be applied in business and life.

If you want to start developing a solution, take some time to deal with the situation where a thoughtful, practical solution should be available. **Start the process with a clear mind.**

1) Create a language change from negative to positive. Think of the "problem" as a "situation." The word problem puts you in a negative mentality from the beginning, while the word situation puts you in a neutral starting point for transformative changes.

2) Clearly define the situation by writing it. Write down the situation from different angles. Ask yourself a series of questions to get an idea of the situation.

3) Ask yourself questions about all possible causes of the situation. The inability to identify the causes or reasons for the situation can sometimes cause a continuous cycle of the situation in your life.

4) Ask yourself and evaluate all possible solutions to the situation. Write as many solutions or answers to the situation as possible before proceeding. The more solutions are possible, the higher the quality of the results.

5) Make a clear decision on your next steps. Making a decision is critical to solving the situation. Note that nothing can be done about the solution. Remember to commit to the decision.

6) Create an action plan for the decision. Includes two dates for completion and review. "

7) Use your action plan to monitor and track your progress, monitor the decision, and compare actual results with expected results. Use this information to generate new solutions and new action plans.

Action phases

1) Clearly write down the problem so that you know exactly what you are planning a solution for. Ask: "What's the problem?"

2) Develop as many solutions as possible. This may include doing nothing. Make sure you don't include anything in your action plan. This should be done before making a decision. The quality of your ideas is directly related to the number of solutions you generate.

The Consequences of Inactivity

You have probably read countless books on how to improve professionally and personally. You may also have attended one or two self-improvement or business improvement seminars. But if you are like most people, despite all this knowledge, your professional and personal life has not changed at all. What went wrong?

As with everything in your life, you have to make a decision. In this case, your choice is clear: apply what you have learned to live a better life or activity or discard that knowledge and stay in your comfort zone?

Understand that action is the key to making positive changes in your life. Without action, knowledge is lost. Inaction does not lead to realization. There is only one obstacle to achieving what is possible: you! If you make the conscious decision to relax and watch the world go by without ever trying to achieve your goals, you will feel a deep regret in your life.

Unfortunately, many people remain inactive in the face of challenges and make the decision to remain in a life of dissatisfaction - to remain in a job that does not bring them satisfaction and to remain in a world of misfortunes. These people are passive in their lives. When opportunities arise, these people do not act. You are not prepared. It is one thing to know what to do; It is quite another to use this information and put knowledge into practice. If you don't take the necessary measures, you will look at the opportunity after opportunity and ask yourself what could have been.

Remember the accompanying focuses when you are prepared to act and genuinely transform you.

1. Don't let fear hold you back.

You cannot let the fear of the unknown or failure prevent you from taking the necessary steps to succeed. You have to stick to your vision, even in difficult times. There is no substitute for persistence! It cannot be replaced by another quality! ... Those who have cultivated persistence seem to protect themselves from failures. Regardless of how often they are defeated, they are finally at the top.

So don't think that the road to success is free of obstacles and challenges. You will surely have difficult moments. But don't let the wrong ideas lull you into inactivity and devour your dreams. Know that despite his needs, he doesn't like all the big hits in his absence. You must be aware and prepared and align your vision with action.

2. Remove the remorse.

The regret you've never tried to get the most out of your potential outweighs the bumps you'll find along the way. There are really no limits to what you can do with your life. Sometimes it's hard to imagine what you won't get out of your life if you don't act. It's a difficult concept for people to think about. However, given the idea of finally doing something, many people quickly make a long list of what could be wrong and why they should stay in their comfort zone. In fact, most people would never run out of reasons when asked why they shouldn't try to do something. However, as soon as you ask them to get an idea of what they expect from life, they suddenly lose their creative abilities.

When it comes to their lifestyle, too many people don't think about what they lose because they never had it. This is the wrong mentality. You can be what you want to be. It is never too late or too early. And don't make mistakes by choosing to stay idle without taking responsibility for what's going on in your life. You give up a lot. Just because you may not be able to touch, it will make you less real.

3. Watch your whole life.

If you are searching for an expert and individual usage, you need to look at the whole picture, your daily life, in its entirety. You will not be able to spend ten hours of your working day and then happily spend the rest of the day, completely forgetting about work. Work is part of life; So to live a full life, work must be part of the general equation. This doesn't mean you can't live a happy life if your job isn't ideal. It simply means that you can make your work part of the wider vision of your life where work is exciting and waiting rather than unrealized and feared.

Try to know yourself. Find your purpose. Try to develop a vision. Develop the goals and plans that translate this vision into reality. And above all, act. Do not stop dreaming. Take the measures that truly define who you are. Separate from those who only talk about things. They are unique and have unlimited potential. These gifts can only be offered to the world if you trade. You should express yourself and bring your talents with you. You will be happy, and this will no doubt be passed on to your fellowmen.

4. Integrate more meaning into your life.

Everyone has moments of happiness that live. If you can add this additional element of meaning, you will move to a higher level. Think about your job. If you don't really care what you do, you don't really care about your job, and it will show it. But how do you behave when you are excited or really interested in the result? Do you behave differently? Do you bet you will? You don't even think about the time or effort it takes to reach your goal. You just do it. It doesn't matter what.

Let's assume you are in the woodwork. Is building a supplement for the aft deck a nuisance? Of course not. Why not because you love it. They can't wait to plan it, get the materials, and you may even have to go to the hardware store, and buy a new tool!

These are not inconveniences. They are requirements, and you don't mind. What if you were asked to set up an animal rehabilitation clinic at the time and had a passion for working with animals? Now you are talking about a real realization. Give up the feeling associated with such a scenario when you settle for a life in everyday life.

Act today

You can discover your purpose, create a vision, and set your goals. However, if no action is taken, it makes no sense. Action is the fundamental component that leads you to a fulfilling life. As obvious as it may seem, acting is the part of the equation that is often overlooked. Nobody will do it for you.

There are three reasons why you need to imagine your dream life. On the one hand, you should clarify what you really want, on the other you should create your destination and the road map to get there, and on the other hand, you should see what you are giving up on if you don't take any action. This does not mean that the life you are living is less valid than someone else's life. It simply means that you are able to make changes and create a life suitable for your purpose.

Think of Earl Nightingale's words: "Success is the gradual realization of a worthy ideal." This is an ongoing process. It will take effort. Acting is hard work, but it can also be fun. That's why it's so important to get involved in something you believe in. Because if you feel you are working hard out of necessity and not out of your free will, you will feel understandably discouraged.

So make the decision to act. You will not regret it.

CHAPTER 10
WHAT KIND OF PROCRASTINATOR ARE YOU?

Procrastinators can be easily divided into four different types of characters. All types are characterized by habitual procrastination and have names known as a poor team player, sorry, potato, and bad as a coward.

Busy bees

They are the people who are often busy like bees. Whenever you talk to them, they are always busy! They always run doing anything except the things they are supposed to do.

They are people who don't understand the difference between doing the right thing and doing the right thing.

Eventually, however, this group of hesitance will never do their job until they are completely exhausted.

The lazy sloth

On the other hand, it is the lazy sloth.

These procrastinators have no sense of urgency or willpower when it comes to doing their thing.

Our willpower is like our muscles. If you don't exercise it, it will atrophy.

You are never motivated to take the first step, even if you never reach the remote control on the TV shelf or the Coca-Cola in the refrigerator.

The main problem with these hesitant is how to start the engine and continue until all the work is done.

Waste of time

Procrastinators with such characteristics simply waste time working on everything except the task required to fulfill their responsibilities. You can spend the whole day cleaning your dog, filing your nails, or combing your hair three times a day, but avoid taking the dog for a much-needed walk.

They invest a great deal of energy chipping away at a particular piece of the movement, but they neglect the whole activity, e.g., Dog grooming. In many situations, they often overlook the most important part of the task and cause great concern for themselves and others who work with them.

Analyzer

As the name suggests, this group of hesitance spends a lot of time analyzing the tasks. Their analysis is usually very superficial and is based on the simplest investigation known to them. They spend a lot of time thinking about how to start working and are even more afraid of the result when they take their first steps. They live more in fear of others, as this explains that they are over-analyzing situations.

All these different types of procrastination mentioned above represent the types of character weaknesses that are within us at one time or another. Some of us are much more of a type and are more important in their actions and behaviors when they work and communicate with loved ones and others.

How can you deal with your weaknesses?

1. The first step is to identify your weaknesses. You can easily solve them with the narrative I provided in the previous part of the section.

2. Next, you need to understand them well, and understanding is a crucial part of your success.

3. It is, therefore, necessary to acquire the appropriate knowledge and measures to deal with it.

4. Finally, take mass measures to keep it under control.

It Helps to Overcome the Delay

Procrastination is one of the most common reasons why people fail to achieve their dreams and goals. But imagine that you can find an easy way to overcome the delay, so you never stop doing the things you need to do to live a happy and fulfilling life.

Indeed, here are a few hints that can assist you with getting over the procrastination:

Do you want, or do you have to?

A big obstacle to achieving your goals is to perceive your daily activities as something you need to do, and not something you want to do. This can often lead to resentment and stress when things are put off at the last minute. One way to overcome the delay is to tell you that you don't have to do anything you don't want to do. From this position, you can evaluate a project on your terms and determine which activities are important for achieving your goals. So you can choose to do it instead of feeling like you should.

Try not to stress about doing things

Sometimes a project seems like a daunting task, and often people don't know how they will ever do it. Try to split the project gradually instead of focusing on the final result. If you take a series of small, manageable steps every day, the project may end before you even get it done.

Stop being a perfectionist

Often, our desire to be perfect in what we do can prevent us from actually doing it. Trying to perform certain tasks while ignoring the details will only hinder your progress. Understanding that nobody is perfect is the key to overcoming the delay.

Remember to have fun

When you're in the middle of an important project, it can sometimes seem like it took your whole life away. This can lead to resentment and / or guilt because you feel that you are missing relaxation or that you are not spending enough time with your family. Here the procrastination can raise its ugly head again! The trick is to plan your time and find a balance between work and leisure. If you allow yourself some time to relax, you can work more productively and are less likely to procrastinate.

These are just a few simple steps to help you overcome the delay in your life. A safe and effective way to overcome the deferment forever is hypnosis. Hypnotherapy has been used effectively by professionals for many years to help people overcome all types of destructive habits, from smoking to overeating. The results are surprising. The good news is that while going to a professional to hypnotize your specific problem, you can now simply listen to audio tapes or download sessions to your computer via MP3 - it's that easy.

Five Ways to Overcome the Delay

Everyone suffers from time to time, including me! There are two types of activities that you procrastinate to do: things you don't want to do and projects that are so close to your heart that you are nervous about doing something about it. These five tips will help you understand why you are hesitant and, more importantly, they will give you some tips to get you going again.

One caveat: all the wisdom, tools and techniques hesitant in the world will not remove the fact that at some point you just have to go in and do it - so if you want to do that moment now rather than later - stop listening to laws and continue with your project!

Tip 1: awareness of resistance

Delay is a manifestation of resistance or deep-seated fear. It is as if we have a gremlin in us, whose only task is to make sure that we are not doing anything mysterious, such as living the purpose of our soul or responding to our true call. Our inner Kremlin wants our lives to be safe, small, and orderly so as not to be hurt by risk or excitement. The Gremlin manifests itself in a perfect way for us. For example, your Gremlin could be the symptoms of the flu you get on the morning you promise to run or the emergency work problem that always arises before planning to attend the evening French lesson to go. Sometimes Gremlin occurs in people around us; for example, your partner or a close relative has a sort of crisis every time you start making progress with your heart's desire.

The behavioral patterns that sabotage are also manifestations of the Gremlin. If you always make the same bad decisions about the relationship, always go looking for good things at work or always go broke before the end of the month, check if this is your Gremlin in action and if it prevents you from being the person you could be.

Awareness of your Gremlin and mysterious functioning is over 50% of the solution. Once you know what's going on, you can start doing something about it.

Tip 2: use your resistance as a compass

If you face obstacles or fears every time you try to take a step forward with your life, calm down from the fact that your inner gremlin will only bow your head when something good happens. There is no resistance to gaining weight on the sofa or spending too many hours in the office. The Gremlin appears only if you improve yourself or pursue a noble goal. Consider his arrival a good thing.

Everyone, including very successful people, suffers from stamina. It is a natural phenomenon of life. However, very successful people continue to act and do their best to keep going despite their stamina: they can't be stopped, and you shouldn't!

Tip 3: Take small steps

It can be daunting to make new efforts or make the

decision to change an unhappy working life. Excitement can soon give way to terror, so procrastination can begin, and progress can stop. The best way to avoid it is to keep the activity steps very small and very simple. If there is something you've put off for a while, break it up into small steps. For example, the thought of "quitting your IT programmer job and becoming a jewelry designer" is very daunting. However, it is much more pleasant to break it down into finding a jewelry design course, converse with someone who is already doing it, or sign up for a test lab. This allows you to make progress towards your dreams without taking drastic measures such as giving up your job dreams and, therefore, your income.

If you take small steps, you can now act without knowing all the details of your plan. This makes the first step manageable and gives you the opportunity to take the following steps step by step. This approach also strengthens your self-esteem so that after a setback (or a Gremlin moment), you can look back on your progress so far and start over in a simple and manageable way.

Tip 4: lower the bar and do it

Sometimes you need to lower the bar and reach your goal rather than setting it too high and not reaching anything. For example, it may not be possible to go to the gym three times a week. However, if you try and actually do it, you will feel good. Isn't it better than always feeling like you're failing?

If you have to do something that you don't want to do, e.g., For example, to tidy, store, or clean, it is best to perform the action for a short period of time (e.g., 15 minutes).

It's more likely to start if you don't have to spend a lot of time on this, and you'll likely find that you will continue a little longer after the start. Alternatively, you can stop after the set time, but set another short goal for another day.

Tip 5: You will do it if the pain of not doing it is greater than the pain of doing it

Ignoring a business or project can cause more problems than before. If you ignore having your stressful job long enough, your health can remind you that everything is not going well. If you postpone taxes long enough, your business will be in even greater chaos, and you will be punished with national revenue.

Waiting for a messy emergency will surely inspire you to act when it finally happens, but isn't it better to do something constructive now?

Six Ways to Overcome the Delay In 10 Minutes A Day

Have you ever been late? Stupid question? Each of us has one time or another! Delay is the number one killer of success. It is the most widespread state that prevents people from acting. It's when you know you should do something, but keep putting it off.

In this section, you will find six ideas that you can immediately apply in your daily life to overcome the delay and do more things in 10 minutes a day.

1) Divide your goals into a number of smaller goals.

If you have a long term goal, divide it into a series of short term goals. By dividing the big objectives into small, reachable steps, a constant sense of realization is experienced. Ultimately, it motivates you to work harder and create a sense of accomplishment every time you reach every goal.

2) Replace negative images in your head with stimulating positive images

Your mind runs with pictures. Do you think what you think of when you work on your goal? Do you feel motivated, inspired, tired, or lazy? Whenever you see negative images in your head, you know that your head associates negative states with your goal.

Identify all the negative images in your head and replace them with motivating images. Think about how exciting, fun, and happy you will be when you reach them all and be successful.

3) Place something useful near your desk

Place something that serves as a source of motivation, e.g., B. inspirational quotes, vision boards, or family photos, right next to the workplace. This simple but effective tip helps destroy the procrastination since it constantly reminds you why you are doing what you are doing.

4) Increase your energy to prevent exhaustion

Being too tired is the main reason for the delay, and your energy reserves (physical and mental) are both limited. Therefore, actively fill them and spread your efforts wisely. Here are some things you can do to increase your energy and prevent burnout:

a) Take some time to train several days a week. Exercise not only helps you reduce stress, but it also strengthens your brain's power, refines your memory, and focuses on work.

b) Reserve the morning and midday hours for the most difficult activities.

c) Take a nap. Research and studies have shown that a 20 to 40-minute nap will significantly improve productivity, creativity, endurance, and work performance.

d) Respect your restrictions. If you are still too tired to take responsibility, reduce your commitments, or get help to fulfill those commitments.

5) Take responsibility for your physiology

If you procrastinated, you used your physiology in a certain way. His breathing was probably slow and shallow. Your muscles were giving way, your eyes were looking down, and probably your face muscles were giving way.

Therefore, adopting your physiology is the key to managing your conditions and overcoming procrastination. You can end the deferment by changing your general physiology. For example, you can sit upright, shoulders back, stretch and take a few deep breaths.

6) Practice "Do It Now" Confirmations

Speaking with your inner voice can be very helpful in quickly overcoming the delay. Whenever you have a goal to achieve, start your thoughts with "Do it now" confirmations. Talk to yourself and say "do it now," "let's do it now" or "let's start." If you do this repeatedly, leave no room for delays in your head.

Remember that the only way you can take control of your time and life is to change the way you think, work, and manage the infinite flow of responsibility that flows over you every day. Practice these simple ideas 10 minutes a day. Check them regularly until they are firmly anchored to your thoughts, and your future is guaranteed.

CHAPTER 11
REACH YOUR GOALS - CREATE AN EDUCATIONAL ENVIRONMENT

Create an environment that is so stimulating and nutritious that it does half the work for you

When your work and living space is cluttered and dirty, when the dishes are stacked in the sink or when your wardrobe is boring, the energy you need to achieve your goals is discharged as if a battery was running out of a forgotten dome light. You need all the energy you need to live your life, and you need to generate more energy to achieve your goals. To do this, make sure that your environment not only meets your requirements (organization, cleaning, maintenance, stock replenishment, etc.) but also make sure that the energy is generated by anticipating your needs and providing reserves. Like? Simple: overcompensation.

For example, if you feel more comfortable with bright colors, don't throw away the black and pick up some nice colored pieces - adjust your wardrobe starting with some neutral primary colors and then the rest Fill the wardrobes with a handful of the brightest items, flattering and elegant that you can afford. In this way, not only will you feel fantastic when you wear them, but when you look in your closet you will feel inspired and excited by everything inside, and you will not be knocked down by going through another "How can I" fight "Throwing something decent from this battle.

If your problem is confusing, organizing and maintaining is a great way to keep it under control. However, you have to do a "Stuff Audit" where you throw away everything (including furniture) that you don't necessarily like or need, and that doesn't match your ideal life ideal - it gives you less of what you need to clean or organize, more space and more emotional energy to dedicate yourself to other activities, as well as the space to move around in selected and deliberately selected objects that inspire and advance you, like great art, a set of really wonderful section knives or the professional one Set of kitchen knives you've always wanted (and never bought because your drawer was already full of lower but reasonably usable knives).

Don't settle for less than you want in life, but less can be more if your new environment supports you, encourages and excites you.

How to Achieve Your Goals: Your Free Guide?

Many of the successful people have now failed before they get where they are now. There are many wealthy businessmen who suffered great losses before they became the extraordinary people they are now. There are also many scientists who have done unsuccessful experiments before becoming famous people they are today. Even famous actors and actresses suffer defeat. Some of them didn't get the roles they auditioned for in the past before they got the roles that gave them the rewards they now enjoy. But the failures didn't stop these people from being successful. They made a special effort to ensure they accomplished their objectives. If you want to get what these people have accomplished, here are some tips on how to achieve your goals.

The first step is to set a specific goal. You need to know exactly what you want and focus on it. There are people who set many goals and think that the more goals they have, the more successful they get. If you do, you will, unfortunately, lose focus on one or two of them, so you will eventually fail.

Although sometimes you may be successful because you are unable to pay enough attention to each, the results are not exactly the best you can get.

Make a plan — set deadlines for all the steps you need to take to achieve your goals. However, make sure the deadlines are realistic.

Ask others for support. Tell your loved ones about your plans so they can help and encourage you.

Mistakes shouldn't stop you from pursuing your goals. Follow these tips to make sure you reach your goals.

CHAPTER 12
FORGIVE YOURSELF

Are there any actions that cannot be forgiven? Never?

From a self-esteem perspective, I suggest that you should always forgive yourself, whatever you have done. The past is in the past, and you cannot change it, but you can change your future. Your future depends on your image of yourself and your relationship with yourself. If you have yourself and consider yourself the worst person in the world, how can you create a good future? Life becomes easier and more fun if you spend it with people you like. You have to spend every second of your life remaining with yourself. If you get mad at yourself for doing something bad, not only your past but your future is doomed to fail.

Of course, if you have committed a serious crime (murder, rape, robbery, etc.), it can be difficult to forgive yourself because society may never forgive you. Even if you spend years in prison to pay for your crime, you may not be forgiven in the eyes of others.

On the other hand, some people find it more difficult to forgive themselves than to forgive others. If you do something that goes against your moral standards (e.g., Disappointing a friend or something like that), it can be difficult to forgive yourself, even if other people don't think you've done something wrong to have.

If you don't forgive yourself, you can't leave the past behind and become a better person in the future. If you can't improve your future, everyone else around you will suffer. You must forgive yourself and continue for yourself and others. A guilty person cannot develop and maintain high self-esteem, but high self-esteem is required to live a good life.

Forgiving yourself is not the same as ignoring what you have done. A person with high self-esteem assumes full responsibility for his or her actions and does everything necessary to prevent bad actions from occurring again. Forgiving yourself is not the same thing as blaming someone else or getting away from your problems.

What is most important for your future, and the future of your fellow humans is that you build a good relationship with yourself. You do this by forgiving yourself and strengthening your self-esteem.

The Three Most Effective Ways to Forgive Yourself

Why is it always easier to forgive others than to forgive ourselves? It seems that we are punishing ourselves for the simplest. All the while, forgiving others who have done much worse for us. How can we forgive ourselves as easily as we forgive others? In this section, you will see the three most effective ways to forgive yourself. OK, let's dive.

First, we must accept in ourselves that we are not perfect and therefore destined to make mistakes from time to time. If we don't forgive ourselves, somehow we think we are superior to everyone else. I believe in high standards, but arrogance and pride will destroy you. Taking responsibility means looking naked, seeing the good, the bad, and the ugly. As uncomfortable as it is, if we make mistakes today, we can make better decisions tomorrow.

Secondly, if you forgive yourself, you must take full responsibility for what happened. Mistakes happen, and if it happens to you, be open and honest. Responsibility for what we do is a true sign of character. Don't run and don't hide if you make mistakes. In this case, the vote may never take place. Instead, talk to those affected to see if peace and trust can be restored. Don't be afraid.

Doing the right thing when it is uncomfortable creates trust and inner strength in us.

Finally, we must learn from the accident and not repeat it. I know it can be painful. I know it could have caused many sleepless nights. But if you learn from these mistakes, you will turn your negatives into a positive. We cannot allow mistakes to judge us. Convince yourself, be honest. If you had the chance to relive the accident, would you change anything?

If you are truly sorry and would not do it again, he will judge an innocent man if you do not forgive yourself.

If you make mistakes, you can feel unworthy of forgiveness. If you follow the previous steps, these feelings can be eliminated. To be as successful as you want, you must be willing to forgive those you have done wrong. And although it is more difficult to forgive yourself, we must do it to live the happy and joyful life that we all desire.

CHAPTER 13
ELIMINATE THE ART OF
PROCRASTINATION

et's face it; Some of us have a reference to art. It doesn't matter what we do; Whether it's work or home business, there will always be some things that we procrastinate or put off. In many cases, we can find all possible ways to avoid it. I think much of this is that we don't have specific reasons for this. We don't attach enough importance to them.

Years ago, I attended a course where they talked about making a list of everything that needed to be done. Try to list everything that has been canceled at home, in your business, and your private life. It takes a long time because there are some things that we mentally classify. They take up space in our brain because we think we should do it at some point, but we rarely write them down. Every time we pass something that reminds us, the feeling of being overwhelmed is intensified. You know when you fall, you can't do anything! ... and then the guilt begins!

You can avoid this overwhelming feeling by listing everything, absolutely everything that needs to be done, and giving it a label. Or immediately, later or at some point, but not now. The "maybe one day not now" allows you to send it and you don't have to think about it because you know it's not urgent. At some point, you will finish the job, but you no longer have to think about it.

Once you have this label for each item, the weight you have crushed will be removed from your shoulders. You can also calmly attack the things that have the highest priority on your list. If you eliminate the art of procrastination, you will get the maximum benefit for the time spent.

Build systems and routines to perform similar or similar activities at the same time every day. This puts you on autopilot, and things are usually done much faster and more consistently. When we grew up, we always had breakfast at eight in the morning, at noon, and in the evening at five. It has become a habit. As children, we only knew that we wanted to eat at that moment, we were sitting at the table at that moment. Whether we were playing outside, we knew we had to be there or lose something if we wanted to eat.

Some instructors say that they should first carry out the most difficult activities. Not always! If you are working on a project that you believe is very, very important, and more difficult to do, be sure to choose the things that will bring you the maximum benefit. Choose an hour of performance, a specific hour of the day, in which you are in activity without distractions. The first things you do in your office for an hour are the things that bring the most reward.

To celebrate success! Some people are oriented toward recognition. Doing something that recognizes the fact that you are making changes will help you maintain or encourage routine. Regulate the things that are important to you emotionally and spiritually.

Set and prioritize the six most important things every night before going to bed. With a set of priorities, do the things that give you the best results. However, the six most important things are not sixty, because putting too many things on a list can hinder you ... You are not updated because you feel overwhelmed again.

Briefly eliminate the art of procrastination:

Create systems and routines

List everything that needs to be done

Prioritize everything with a specific date or a "Maybe now" ... "Maybe a day, but not now."

The six most important things are listed every night

Adhere to a certain time of the show every day

Celebrate your success

The feeling of having achieved something or being satisfied, if you stick to something consistently, see the pile of tasks go down, and the rewards pile up is amazing. Take a look at what you can put off for a long time, and you don't have to think about what to face today and start because you will see that the results are spectacular.

CHAPTER 14
GET OVER THE DELAY BY UNDERSTANDING WHY YOU'RE DELAYING

In the classic procrastination, important tasks remain incomplete until the last minute. For this reason, procrastinators tend to miss appointments and cause problems for themselves. Overcoming procrastination is possible if you want to understand why people postpone.

Everyone has the skills to be organized and efficient. We were not born procrastinators. Delay is learned over time and develops in our lives. Once this behavior is rooted in us, we must fight to fight it to be productive. You must choose to overcome the delay to avoid personal and professional problems in our lives.

Those who procrastinate often do not take responsibility for putting their duties aside. The first step in overcoming this problem is to understand that the problem is hesitation. Many people know what needs to be done to get a job. However, they avoid it but make an apology. They often use their busy schedule as a reason for not managing something. You can start many projects, but they don't follow.

Some procrastinators are afraid of failure, so difficult tasks are often not done. If you feel you are confusing a business, keep putting it aside. Some people will delay a project without trying it first. To overcome the delay, you must stop living in denial. To do this, you must recognize that you are responsible for your life.

Overcoming procrastination takes a lot of time and effort. Don't tell yourself that being productive is not for you. Just buckle up and do whatever you hinder.

Five Steps to Overcome The Delay

Millions of people struggle to achieve goals and overcome challenges due to the habit of delay. It is one of the most generally perceived individual issues with which people search for help. There are a few reasons why individuals put off or stay away from exercise. They can go from basic essential lethargy to dread of disappointment, absence of trust in your capacities, or just a solid hatred of the undertaking.

People usually avoid doing things because they don't know what to expect or what the outcome might be. They may fail; others may laugh at them; they may seem silly; there may be a lot of stress or any number of non-specific fears. Every day we struggle with the fear of the unknown. It is the way we think and our perception of the things that paralyze us and keep us in an avoidance scheme. If you think something is inconvenient or uncomfortable, or that you fail when you try to do it, or if you think you are missing something, you will probably make sure you never get there. In most cases, this creates a high level of stress or unpleasant circumstances.

When you come into contact with the pain you feel when you procrastinate, you can take the first step to overcome it.

Many people procrastinate because of a lack of motivation. To combat this delay, you can set up rewards for doing these unwanted things. If training is difficult, reward yourself every time you go to the gym. You deserve to resist. Next time you may be much more motivated.

For many people, putting off daily life takes a long time. Because of this habit, they fail to do things. This leads to more stress and more frustration. In the end, putting things off makes things much more difficult than if you just do the job. If you stop the delay, you can avoid any pain caused by the failure of the delay.

Other reasons why people procrastinate:

Lack of confidence in one's abilities

Afraid to try something new because it has failed in the past

Low self-esteem

The goal is not linked to a reward

Procrastination is one of the most time-consuming activities. It causes a lot of stress and frustration. Here are five steps you can use to defer procrastination easily.

Step 1: find your direction.

Whenever you procrastinate, write down the task to avoid and your justification for avoiding it. By keeping records, you can better understand how your attitudes relate to your procrastination. So you can identify strategies for redirecting yourself when you feel the need to postpone something. Always focus on the task you want to do and your reward if you are successful. Focusing on reward is the most effective way to overcome delays.

Step 2: concentrate

You can, without a ton of a stretch, be overpowered on the off chance that you try to do it all the while. Rather, isolate your objectives into less difficult assignments. Put them vigorously individually. Start as ahead of schedule as could be allowed. Require some serious energy consistently to take a shot at your objectives. If you experience issues beginning a business, take a shot at it for ten minutes. This will, as a rule, assist you with getting some energy, and you will feel like you are pushing ahead. First, start with a simple task and imagine how you can do the business. This will help you focus on the goal and the reward you will receive on completion.

"Most people have no idea of the enormous capacity we can have immediately if we focus all our resources on mastering a single area of our life." -Tony Robbins

Step 3: be aware of your thoughts.

The more you procrastinate, the more monumental the task becomes in your head. Allowing restrictive beliefs to control your actions becomes a parasite of your chances of success. You have to compare your beliefs about yourself and the task and face your fears. Instead of dreaming about your failure and all the things that could go wrong and how difficult it will be, imagine how good you will feel when you have completed the activity and how safe you will feel when you do it complete them and how confident you can do the next. Maintain your positive concentration, and this will build a new position that overcomes all your limiting beliefs and defeats the delay.

Find out how to separate your scary thoughts from your realistic thoughts. Imagine the worst-case scenario. So make a plan to get back on your feet in case the worst happens. You would probably recover quickly enough and resume a normal life.

"Our attitude toward life determines our attitude towards us." -John N. Mitchell

Step 4: build your tolerance for negative emotions.

Anxiety and stress are normal. They come from being insecure or feeling threatened in some way. Most of the time, they are just feelings, and there is no real danger. Courage is not the absence of fear, but the ability to continue despite everything. Courage is needed to overcome the delay.

If you continue to pursue your goals, you will build your tolerance for stress and anxiety. Over time, you will feel safer, more efficient, and much less stressed and overwhelmed. You don't fear the feelings of anxiety, and you will procrastinate less.

Meditation is an effective way to resist negative emotions. Large universities around the world have found that it reduces stress and anxiety, improves mood, and improves concentration.

Step 5: Take command of yourself.

Success always means leaving the comfort zone. No matter how uncomfortable the result of procrastination is, the habit remains part of your comfort zone. A very important first step is to stop complaining about what you need to do. Nothing worthwhile is easy, and when you complain, you lose the will to succeed. Focus on all the benefits you get when you're successful, whatever you need to do. Focus on how wonderful you will feel and what wonderful things will happen to you if you are successful.

"Self-control is the main discipline." -Ralph Waldo Emerson

Getting over the delay isn't as difficult as you might think. Once you take these five steps to overcome the delay, your fears and fears will disappear, and you will experience the many benefits of being in control of your life.

CHAPTER 15

HOW TO STOP THE PROCRASTINATION - EFFECTIVELY AND EFFICIENTLY

Delay can ruin your life. Constant delays in completing activities can lead to stress, missed opportunities, disappointments, and a reputation for failure. You could become a failure.

With the real possibilities mentioned above, the question resounds loudly: what is the most effective way to overcome the delay in the shortest possible time? My research on personal and social improvement has led to the following result.

It is vital to understand why you are reluctant to start or run a specific business or project. Only when you know the exact cause of your particular delay can you honestly start solving the problem. And you don't solve the problem by attacking the problem, but attacking the cause of the problem with the opposite of the cause.

Keep that thought in mind. Solve a problem by identifying the cause and then attacking the cause with the opposite.

In the event of deferral, there are only four reasons why a person unnecessarily delays completing an activity or project.

 # 1 - Work Overload - You feel overwhelmed by other activities and cannot find the time to start the activity. Solution: reduce or delay the least advantageous responsibilities and create the necessary time. Find the cause again and attack the opponent.

 # 2 - Anxiety - You are afraid to start the project because you believe it will cause physical or emotional pain or discomfort. Solution: divide the project into comfortable (or at least painful) parts and face it segment by segment. If you act somewhat coherently, the activity is complete.

 # 3 - Resentment - You refuse to carry out the activity because you believe it has been imposed on you or that it should be carried out by someone else. Solution: Be man or woman enough to advertise your resentment and see if you can find the most suitable person to do the job. If this approach doesn't work, you have no choice but to use the strategy outlined in step 2 above.

 # 4 - Overwhelmed - You feel overwhelmed by the project because you are not sure how to do it. Solution: gain knowledge. There is hardly anything you can face that someone else doesn't have. They wrote about it or are ready to talk about how they got over it.

Finally, keep in mind that we only procrastinate concerning something we don't want to do (for any reason). If we want to do something, it will be done. Therefore, identify the advantages of completing the project and not the disadvantages associated with completing the activity or project. This mental trick works even if the only advantage is that you no longer have to worry about the unfinished project.

Remember, you can't overcome a bad habit like postponing by attacking the problem yourself. Instead, it is necessary to identify the mental or emotional cause of the problem and attack the cause in reverse. This doesn't mean you can simply think about how to get out of the delay. Action must follow thought.

change

CHAPTER 16
THE REAL COST OF PROCRASTINATION FOR SECURITY-CONSCIOUS PEOPLE

Postponing security can be very expensive. This is because, in areas where potential hazards can cause accidents, safety should be a top priority regardless of the total cost. In some workplaces, it is common for employers to take safety for granted and that their employees take care of their safety. They tend to forget that, as employers, they are directly responsible for the safety of all workers who work under or over their roofs. Postponing security can entail the following obvious and not so obvious costs;

Bridging the gaps - For example, if you work in high places and do not install fall protection systems at strategic points along the roof and its periphery, dangerous gaps can occur in which the worst accidents can occur in the least expected moments.

In other cases, the loopholes may not be very obvious until an accident has reported their presence. To reduce the costs of accidents, these voids must be identified and closed in good time.

Public image - Companies that want to strengthen their public image and look professional must know which security systems to use, especially when their employees run public contracts. This means that tools and equipment must be updated and in perfect condition. Care should be taken to ensure that their employees exercise the necessary care to ensure that they are always safe and can do their job comfortably. How the public considers a company determines how much activity it should do at a given moment. Today security speaks to the public.

Accident tendency: A company can't know which of its employees has a higher accident tendency. This is because all people have different mental and physical abilities and react very differently in different circumstances. For example, workers in workplaces where fall protection systems such as roof anchors are designed for their height safety would react very differently.

Attitude: security and personal attitude are closely related. In places where safety is not repeatedly emphasized, workers can tend to be more negative than in places where safety is increased. This can be seen from the general quality and quantity of the work, as well as the frequency and severity of the accidents. Lack of adequate security affects the way workers view their employers, and employers who want to keep their workers satisfied and satisfied must take care of their safety. A negative employee attitude is very expensive for any company.

Unrest - In the long run, workers are very likely to become restless if safety is taken for granted. For example, if employers do not guarantee adequate ladder safety, many falls can be reported in high places. If these are not handled properly, workers tend to feel troubled because they feel exposed to accidents every time they work in high places. This vulnerability could lead to hostility from the employer and, in case of prolonged suppuration, finally industrial actions. The effects of industrial action can be far-reaching and very damaging to any company wishing to continue its long-term business.

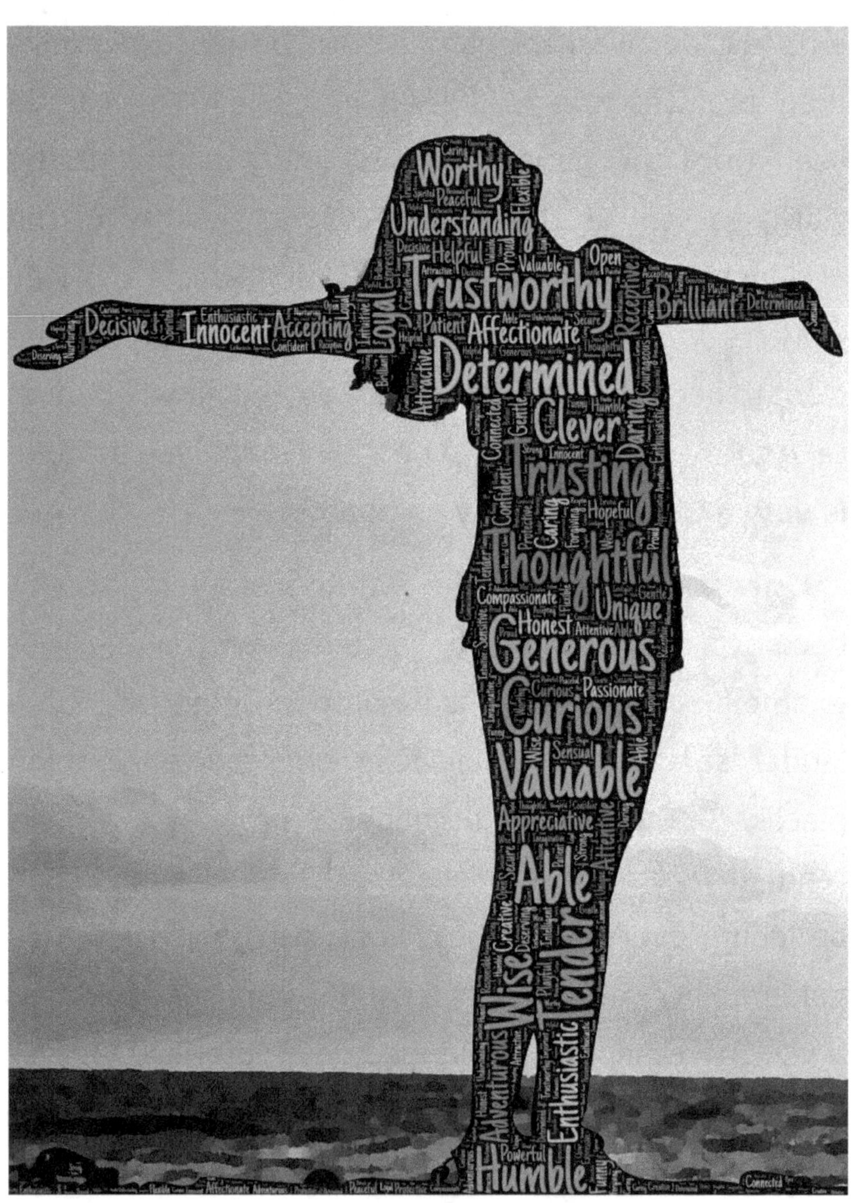

CHAPTER 17

THE MOST IMPORTANT THINGS EVERYONE SHOULD KNOW ABOUT PROCRASTINATION

Maybe you have a procrastination problem.

Many people are affected by the vice, and although they make a lot of effort to no longer be a procrastinator, it seems impossible to get rid of it. This is because people are trying to overcome the problem instead of overcoming the cause. Read on for some of the main procrastination causes.

Fear makes people procrastinate. If you are uncertain of what you need to do or in the event that you have a feeling of inadequacy, procrastination is likely to occur. If you are also worried that something bad will happen before you do the job, you will probably procrastinate in fear.

If you don't sort things by importance, you can't offer what you expect. You certainly have a lot to do, but some are more important than others. If you do not have a priority list, "activity overload" is likely to occur. If you have several things to do but have not yet set a schedule, you probably won't even start anything. Organize yourself now so that you are no longer a procrastinator.

Some people are generally afraid of success because they are not sure what others will think of them. You will always postpone the beginning. These people can use Emotion Freedom techniques if they want to stop being procrastinators and want to realize that success is good and possible for them. Therefore, you shouldn't be afraid to start any business.

Stress is also very common. When a lot of pressure builds up in your body in the form of stress, it can help you get sick. As a rule, this can lead to a decrease in performance and, therefore, a poor quality of work. People with accumulated internal pressure need therapeutic help to overcome the habit of procrastination. Pressure from others can also be a big reason for the procrastination. If others make you feel like you are unable to do the job or if you are better than yourself, you may simply procrastinate and not start the job you wanted to do in a certain period.

If you don't have the motivation to do the homework in front of you, you probably won't do it. You can also get bored in the middle of work.

All these problems are the main causes of deferral and can be solved using EFT techniques. If you are looking for the best way to stop procrastinating, you can also think of emotional freedom techniques. The moment you know how to defeat these behaviors, you have overcome the delay.

The Lame Thing of The Procrastination

Sometimes most of us will procrastinate. We will put off things we know we shouldn't and find all sorts of plausible excuses for not doing something we should have done. Here are a bit of the most exceedingly fearful things about procrastination. Discover which one suits you best.

It was not enough time

If you believe it, you will believe everything. Unless the deadline for the 30,000-word report is 5 minutes, the time is almost always sufficient. The problem is that we are good at finding things that are related to our time, and that doesn't solve the problem. Check your emails or Facebook every two minutes. Prepare and drink another cup of coffee. Watch the news with the possibility of finding something worth talking about. The list of excuses for not doing something rarely ends, and there is almost always one that we can use as an excuse to procrastinate.

Don't plan (or plan to fail)

Our procrastination is often the result of not worrying about planning. It's okay to plan out-of-the-ordinary things, and everything you do routinely will probably have enough plans. But other things deserve the courtesy of planning, especially if they can influence other people. It might appear glaringly evident; however, how often have you neglected to design something, and afterward, you understood that you don't have everything to do what you needed. The result is synonymous with hesitation and procrastination. Also, in this case.

Planning to procrastinate

There are probably not too many people who would admit it. But if you are an experienced procrastinator, various delay tactics may be a natural part of your daily routine. You know the dog ate my homework, and you might even have a small notebook with you, so you don't stumble too often at the funeral of the same dead relative.

Look at the watch

If your reaction is "Oh, well, I'm running out of time" even if you haven't done the job, it's likely that, deep down, you will have fun putting things off until tomorrow. Sometimes it's okay - sometimes we need the ability to think about something instead of just opening our big mouth. But sometimes it annoys everyone around us who has to come to the rescue (if we don't deliver on time).

Screwing up our priorities

Some things have a higher priority than others. This should be obvious, but it often happens that we give the choice of the type of cake we eat with our Starbucks a higher priority than this important task that we set ourselves the other day. If you have difficulty determining the priority of an activity that has been set, contact the person who assigned the activity to you. And if they have no idea, decide for yourself that this is actually a low priority and deliberately procrastinate.

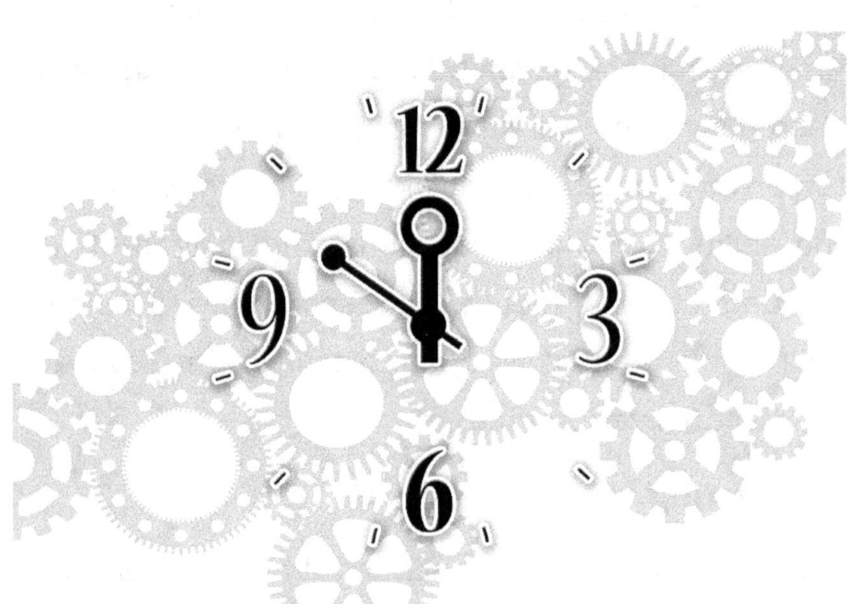

CHAPTER 18
SELF-TALK

Most of the time, we convince ourselves that we are good while doing the worst possible actions. Imagine that suicide bombers kill hundreds and are still convinced that they will go to heaven. A man cheats on the cards. He convinces himself to think that his opponents are not worth playing fairly. Like a horn, a peacock's tail, and a general swelling, we will believe in our manufacture ... we will not shy away. And our overconfidence could intimidate opponents. As humans, we have a somewhat more sophisticated means of inflating ourselves than our animal counterparts.

Self-deception is a process or fact that causes us to accept claims about us as true (valid) when they are false (invalid). If we justify false beliefs about ourselves, we must convince ourselves of truth (or lack of truth) so as not to reveal self-knowledge to deception. Self-deception is a useful strategy for believing in the stories we tell. If we succeed, we will be less likely to shy away and accidentally report that we are different from what we pretend to be. An unjustified increase in self-confidence ... can increase our general well-being by helping us manage stress. It can increase our endurance in difficult or long tasks. It can lead us to have new and different experiences.

When our fellow humans and we are dishonest, we begin to suspect everyone, and without trust, our lives become more difficult. Of course, it's exciting to be bright and hope for a wonderful future - but in the case of self-deception, our exaggerated beliefs can destroy us when reality falls. However, the obscurity of our true motivations does not prevent us from creating perfectly logical reasons for our actions, decisions, and feelings. We want explanations about why we do this and how the world around us works. As natural narrative creatures, we tell each other by the story until we find an explanation we like, and that sounds reasonable enough to believe. And if history presents us in a brighter and more positive light, all the better.

We are divided by a fundamental conflict: our profound propensity to lie to ourselves and to others and the desire to consider ourselves good and honest people. We justify our dishonesty by telling stories about why our actions are acceptable (even admirable). People committed crimes based on a rational analysis of each situation. One day Becker was late for a meeting and decided to park illegally and risk a ticket due to the limited number of legal parking spaces. Becker noted that his decision was about weighing imaginable costs - caught, punished, and perhaps towed - against the advantage of getting to the meeting on time. He also noted that when evaluating costs and benefits, there was no place to think right or wrong, but only the comparison of possible positive and negative results.

And that's how the Simple Model of Rational Crime (SMORC) was born. We all think and behave similarly to Becker, according to this model. We are all committed to our advantage as we make our way around the world.

However, dishonesty is not the result of a simple consideration of the costs and benefits of dishonesty. We always want to see ourselves as honest, honorable people ... the "ego motivation." But we also want to benefit from the fraud and get as much money as possible ... "financial motivation." The two are obviously in conflict. How can we guarantee the benefits of fraud while considering ourselves as an honest and wonderful person? Thanks to this human ability, as long as we cheat a little, we can take advantage of cheating and still consider ourselves wonderful people. This balancing act is the process of rationalization and the basis of the so-called "melting factor" theory. We all try to find out where we can benefit from dishonesty without damaging our image of ourselves.

If we want to eradicate crime, we need to find a way to change the way we can rationalize our actions. As our ability to rationalize our selfish desires increases, we feel more comfortable with our illicit and deceptive actions. The other side is also true; When we are less able to rationalize our actions, our "confusion factor" narrows, making us less comfortable with incorrect behavior and cheating. When we look at the range of unwanted behaviors in the world, honesty and dishonesty are much more than rational calculations. As long as we cheat a little, we can enjoy the benefits of dishonesty while maintaining a positive image of ourselves.

Remember that one percent of people will always be honest and will never steal. Another percentage is always dishonest and tries to break the lock, and the rest will be honest as long as the conditions are right -----, but if they are tempted enough, they will also be dishonest. Locks don't protect you from thieves ... they can break into your homes if they're serious. Locks protect you from mostly honest people who would be tempted to test your door if it didn't have a lock.

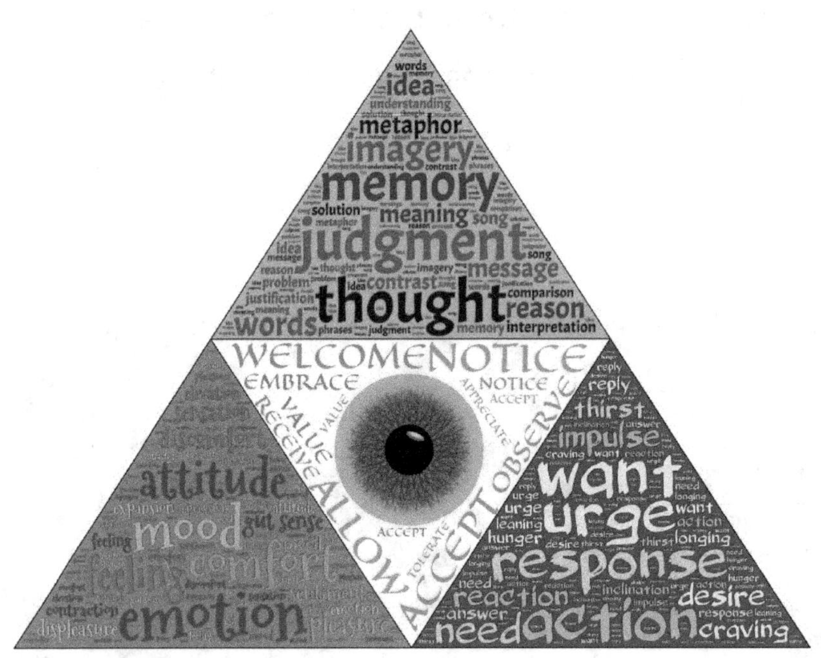

words
idea
understanding
metaphor
imagery
memory
solution
meaning song
judgment
idea message song
reason
problem thought idea contrast imagery message
justification
words phrases judgment thought reason comparison
memory interpretation
WELCOME NOTICE
EMBRACE NOTICE
ACCEPT
VALUE RECEIVE APPRECIATE OBSERVE
ACCEPT
ALLOW ACCEPT
attitude
mood gun sense
feeling comfort
feeling
contraction
displeasure emotion
reply
reply
thirst
impulse
craving want reaction
want
urge urge
leaning want action
hunger longing
response thirst
need inclination desire
reaction
answer action need action craving
need action craving

CHAPTER 19
THE POWER OF GETTING STARTED

Stop the apology, and get started!

"Little spirits are tamed and subdued by misfortune, but great spirits rise above them." - Washington Irving

I'm sorry he's a purpose killer. There are and are increasing reasons why you should not do what a turnaround could bring to your life. It stops you in your lane. Kill your dreams and leave a miniature in the wild ocean of life. The truth is, you have a thousand reasons why you shouldn't go any further. Everyone is inclined to apologize, but it's up to you not to get involved. After studying the lives of successful people, I found that everyone decided to work against the tides. They have every reason not to do what ultimately led to their success, but they contradicted popular opinion and did it differently. I'm sorry it's a harbinger of failure. It puts a wall between you and your dreams. So you have to quit. It can develop into a serial chain of problems, overshadowing your life ambition.

There are general excuses that people can't achieve a certain result. Some think they are too young and lose an idea that could change their life. Even if I sign up early, being old is not an excuse for not realizing your life dreams. Many stories in history indicate this fact. Tell me some interesting parts of people who would have preferred to apologize for their failure and have become great icons:

Winston Churchill failed in first grade. He was subsequently defeated in every public office election until he became prime minister at the age of 62.

Thomas Edison's educators said he was "too dumb to even think about learning." He was terminated from his initial two occupations because "not beneficial." As an innovator, Edison made 1,000 fruitless endeavors to develop the light. At the point when a correspondent asked, "What was it like to bomb multiple times?" Edison answered, "I haven't bombed multiple times. The light was an innovation with 1,000 stages."

Henry Ford fizzled and bombed multiple times before he succeeded

R. H. Macy failed multiple times before his business in New York turned into a triumph.

Walt Disney was terminated from a paper editorial manager since "he needed a creative mind and had a whole lot of nothing thoughts." He failed several times before building Disneyland. Indeed, the proposed park was rejected by the city of Anaheim because it would only attract Riffraff.

Beethoven was embarrassed with the violin and preferred to play his compositions rather than improve his technique. His educator called him "miserable as a writer." What's more, you realize he composed five of his greatest orchestras while he was totally hard of hearing.

I can go on forever. Your physical disability shouldn't stop you from being what you're meant for. You can turn your disadvantage into strength and find a means of expression for your goals. Some argue that they are already disadvantaged because they come from poor backgrounds and, as such, cling only to what life has to offer. No wonder why they will never excel in life. Your apologies may be logical, but they are not the truth. You need to develop enough willpower to move forward. It must be on purpose. Let's see how we can deal with this monster called sorry:

Shut up, and I can't whisper: this attitude gives you no reason to doubt that you can get what you have decided to do. It completely closes your heart to all available options and blinds your eyes on the image that you are the best. Sometimes these whispers are very subtle; They come in other varieties such as "Nobody has ever done this in your family or nation or even in the world and what makes you think you can." Unfortunately, many of us have succumbed to this blackmail.

Enter the realm of "I can" - Scripture says: "Nothing will be impossible for those who believe." - Matthew 17:20. The scriptures make it clear that nothing is impossible. All you need is to believe and leave to reach it. Always move into the realm of "I can" and see how fast your life will turn. It is always a devil lie that you feel like you are not up to the task.

Put on the "I'll do it" cloak - There is a fine line between the "Can" area and wear the "I'll do it" cloak, and that's the decision. The "I can" realm offers you the options available to help you achieve your goals, while the "I want" realm is that you choose a course from the available options and work through them. If you choose, you managed to throw that excuse into the coffin.

Put on the boot of "I Am" - here "bury" your apologies. The decision is not enough. You must be a culprit. It is not only the planners who are justified but those who execute the plans. You must wear the 'I Am' boot because the ride can be tough and difficult. You can deal with the "Red Sea," and you may be tempted to slip into "I can't," but don't give up. Others have already followed this path, and if not, then congratulations, because your name will be a pioneer of gold.

Receive the "I Did" medal - this is the reward you will receive at the end of the obstacles. This is the image you think as you make your way into the realm of "I can" and do you know what? You earned the medal because you paid the price to come here. You imagined it, and now you are there. There is no limit to what you can get. Stretch your mind and watch what you see. God bless you, big.

QUESTION
everything

CHAPTER 20
PROCRASTINATION - IT LOOKS LIKE A DUCK!

You know the saying: "If it looks and looks like a duck, it's probably a duck."

Well, this way of thinking may be excellent for wise minds sitting on their rocking chairs, but it's not very useful when trying to run a business.

The "duck" in this case are the behaviors that make you appear and sound like you are "hesitating," and therefore, you MUST be "hesitant." Judgment formulated, case closed.

Of course, this doesn't help you act. Labeling worsens the situation. My name is Douglas Cartwright, and I train people on how to loosen their psychological "knots" and how to become more effective.

I want to show you some perspectives about what could happen if we delay something and suggest some resources to help.

1) Some people believe that the brain always tries to do something positive for us (although it may not be morally good) and that it is positive to protect us from danger. This danger cannot be the fear of being physically injured, but the fear of being psychologically injured: the fear of failure and what others will think.

2) Susan Jeffers, who wrote the famous Feel the Fear and Foul anyway, says that the basic fear behind all fears is unable to deal with it.

One of the reasons why we feel we can't make it is overwhelming, and although the advice to break things down is known, the reason is not. Anything that is perceived as a threat activates the combat or flight response. The solution is to take small steps that do not awaken the centers of fear. The book A Little Step Can Change a Life is easy and excellent if you think this is your problem.

3) If you come from a place where you think work should be hard, you can avoid "dirt" and "tingling" if you can. Now Habit by Neil Fiore offers an excellent and radical solution to this problem: plan your free time first! It is also recommended to work only for ½ hour. When you have done this, you can mark it on the empty spaces in your program AND reward yourself. If you like something different and other time management books have not worked for you, you can make it worse.

Say Goodbye to The Procrastination with This Three-Step Process

"What if I could say goodbye to deferment forever?" In all honesty, there is an approach to do it!

You can say "goodbye!" this! It may seem "too easy," but it's really that simple - simple, but very effective! What I'm suggesting is that you learn to "Outsource it!"

Try this three-step process to outsource, eliminate and determine

Step 1: outsource it!

Therapeutic outsourcing means making a mental projection in the form of an image outside of yourself, and it is a consulting method that is used in narrative therapy. It is a very useful therapeutic "tool" to reduce self-accusation and allows customers to make room to reformulate and restructure their identity. Therapists and consultants can adapt their use of outsourcing to a much broader spectrum, as they are when I question your current vision of "procrastination."

Often we don't call him directly by name, more often we talk about it indirectly or think about it (e.g., "I should do it, but ..." or "It doesn't seem like he's coming to this project, maybe later." .. ") just to ask "why" we can't achieve our goals. We know we "hate" him and "we want him to go," but it seems that we certainly have not become great experts when it comes to saying goodbye finally.

So if you see "Procrastination" (I'm using it now because it has become an "It" with a name!) As an entity outside of you ... someone else or something else ... can help you a lot to overcome the feelings of "I am a" bad "procrastinator or something. When you outsource, you essentially relieve yourself of the weight because the" procrastinator "or" procrastination "is out of you ... you are not! That is, the next time you have problems with time management, and you feel that procrastination controls your actions, you can stop blaming yourself and sabotage your self-confidence to change your behavior. I'm not "The Procrastinator" and "The Procrastinator" is not your identity! Period.

Perhaps you see it this way: "Now I am learning that the procrastination can no longer be in my life and that my decisions are no longer made for the benefit of the procrastination! It is me, and now it must go!" Take a picture of the procrastination (create some vision in your mind's eyes) and watch the procrastination go through a door and out of your life. "

When you outsource "procrastination," you can let it go and the inner grip it once had on you. The procrastination no longer has to be your arch enemy. If you try to consider it separate from yourself, you can start to gain the upper hand, free from the frustration it has brought. But the work doesn't stop there.

Step 2: eliminate resistance

Once you decide to release him, you must start eliminating his partner, the Resistance. Much of your hesitant behavior is based on "mental endurance." So it makes sense to find a way to make room for a new way of thinking. Now you can also repeat step 1 and outsource "Resistance" ("Now" also has a name). Let me go through the same door as Procrastination!

The bottom line is that you have fought two tough opponents, and it seems that the more "we resist," the more we procrastinate, and the stronger "resistance and procrastination" becomes and seems to take precedence over our existence. How do you fight resistance?

Use affirmations to remove resistance. Use your words and take action to achieve this. For example, you could say "I no longer allow resistance and procrastination to rent space in my head and use my mental energy" or "I am watching resistance and procrastination leave me now," or you may take a slightly different approach and say " I am free to choose procrastination and endurance as friends (or perhaps as teachers) so I can learn more about why they detained me, and I have struggled with them and myself to get things done! "

To eliminate resistance, you must be very aware of your presence. It's sneaky if you're not careful. Resistance makes your body terrible.

Every reaction you have to a negative feeling is your body's attempt to send you the "red flag" that is moving. What you may or may not notice is that you can check your "resistance meter," and if you don't want resistance, you can let your thoughts get past you. Use your words again and say, "I'm scared right now, and this tells me that the Resistance is trying to get back into my life or home. There's no place for you, Resistance. I'm here in peace without you "The more you say and believe and feel it, the more you can lower your heart rate, and the fear will dissipate.

To take this one step further, resistance is a byproduct of fear. Fear is not so easy to outsource, so we need to broaden the search for answers by looking at the underlying fear that triggered your resistance and caused procrastination and resistance to rent space in your head.

Step 3: determine your fear

Ask yourself what the last time you heard when resistance led to hesitant behavior was. Did you feel anxious, scared, confused, frustrated, angry? Think about it and try to deepen the process of your hesitant behavior. Step 3 is an important part of this puzzle. **First, consider the following three questions:**

1. Am I afraid of being rejected by others when I achieve this goal or task?

2. I'm afraid I don't know all the answers, so is it better not to take the initiative than to try to fail?

3. I am afraid to let go of the delay because it protected me, and if I voluntarily give up something that has become precious to me, wouldn't I feel lost without it?

This should trigger personal introspection if you want to look for the source of your fear. Remember: "Your fear led to your resistance that made procrastination possible." It is never easy to look inside and become aware of negative feelings and behaviors. However, if you start this process by letting go of your identity as "The Procrastinator" or "A Procrastinator," you have taken the first big step in learning how to "outsource, eliminate and determine" your success!

Why Procrastination Can Be Very Dangerous to Health

If you find yourself repeatedly delaying important tasks, you are not alone. Many people have procrastinated in several ways, but some are constantly affected by the delay that prevents them from meeting their prospects and affects their performance.

Delay is as tempting as it is painful. If you think

you're hesitating, you need to find out why you're doing it. And if you know the reason for your delay, you may want to know how to defeat it.

Examples of deferral situations

A basic case of a slacker is an understudy who doesn't have a clue how to organize things and his calendar. He would invest a lot of energy if he pretended to play or doing a long-distance film race, and he doesn't care that there will be a semester exam next week. He would postpone his schedule, again and again, you know, I'll make it a habit tomorrow. And when the day before his semester comes, it's time to scan and fill the pages of his notes. He would say to himself now or never, or at least I read, right? The result is obvious, and it will fail. After that, he would blame himself.

Another situation is that an employee who resigned from his job several times because he was unable to complete a task felt very stressed and ill. Her life was full of half-started and half-finished projects, which gave her the impression of being very incompetent and irresponsible for her work. The stress was incredible in that it severely affected his performance, his life at home, and indeed every part of his life. The delay kills her, and she urgently needed to find a cure for this.

Reasons why procrastination hurts

Here are some reasons why procrastination can be harmful to you and very dangerous to your health.

Personal circumstances

Do you know that procrastination is not good for your personal life? If you repeatedly repeat household chores or duties in a relationship, e.g., B. washing dishes or cooking, removing and disposing of garbage, married life, and other relationships may be affected.

You can then find that procrastination is downright negative if your relationship with your spouse is on the verge of things you haven't taken seriously.

It does not give you inner peace

Another reason why procrastination is negative is that it takes away your inner peace. I'm always late for appointments or meetings. Always run outside the door, make up the car, call or write messages while you are driving, and risking your life and those people with you. Postponing appointments to the dentist may seem easy. However, once your cavity gets worse, and you miss a working day with your significant sales presentation, drop that customer and your promotion expectations, and you would see why there are delays is not a good thing

It affects your reliability factor

Yes, hesitation hurts your reliability or credibility. If your girlfriend needs something from you, your character may be so mistreated that she doesn't rely on you to do a job when she needs you. Her best friend may have fallen ill and will have to take her son from kindergarten. However, he might think twice before asking you a favor because he knows you're not on time or undecided until school is almost over.

Overcoming the Procrastination

Here are the steps you can take to manage and control the delay:

Step 1: Recognize that you are hesitating

The following symptoms and signs will help you recognize when you are hesitating:

- You usually fill the day with low priority tasks.

- Read emails repeatedly without knowing how to change them or what to do with them.

- Skip an item in the to-do list for a long period,

even if you know it's important.

- Sit in front of the computer or desk to do a priority task, and you will go out to prepare a cup of tea almost immediately.

Regularly accept unimportant activities that others would like to do and spend your time instead of working on the important activities that are already on your list.

- Usually, wait for the right moment or mood to complete the essential activity.

Step 2: find out why you're hesitating

- Uncomfortable or boring work can sometimes be the reason for your delay in trying to avoid it. Finish quickly so you can continue and focus on the most pleasant aspects of the activity.

Another reason could be that you are not organized. The best way to manage it is to create and prioritize your to-do lists and schedules.

Perfectionists tend to be procrastinators because they believe they don't have the skills or resources to do the job perfectly, so in the end, they don't.

Step 3: adopt deferral strategies

Delay is a difficult habit to eliminate. Here are some useful reasons to keep you going:

• You have to put together your rewards, just like you promise yourself a piece of delicious chocolate cake for dessert when you have completed a certain task. Make sure you are aware of how good it is to get things done.

Peer pressure works. You can ask a companion or partner to look at you. This is considered to be the principle of support groups and is generally considered to be a highly effective approach.

• You need to be aware of the consequences of not doing the job.

So this is the anger of the procrastination. It is very harmful to your efficiency, dangerous for your health, too stressful, and can often be very frustrating for your friends and colleagues. If you think you are a procrastinator, then you need, and you MUST hit it right away. So do what you have to do today and do it now.

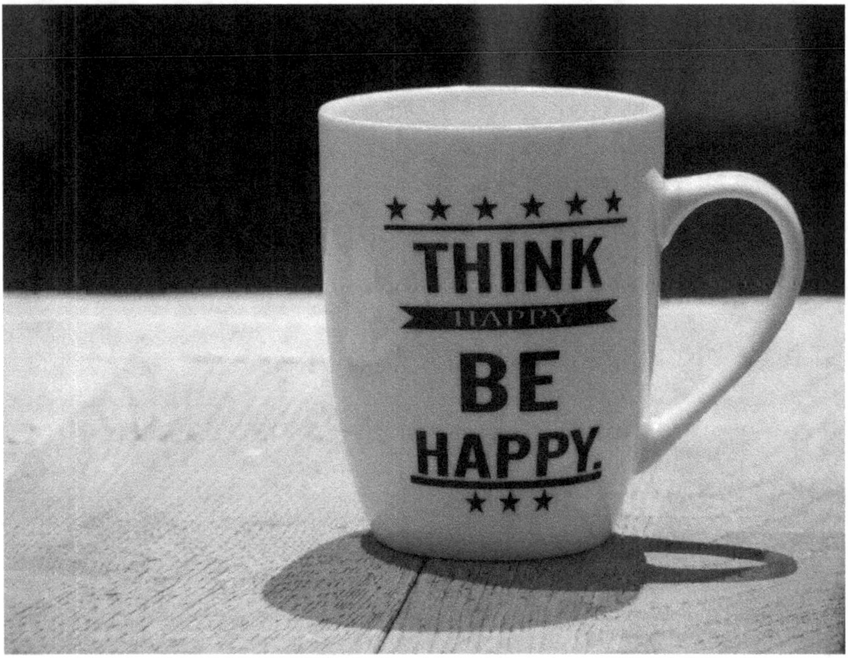
THINK
HAPPY
BE
HAPPY.

CONCLUSION

Protect Yourself from Procrastination

A watch can break, but time doesn't stop. Inspired by these words, say to yourself: "I will think about this idea for a while. Later I will use my time efficiently and effectively." (This conditional deferral is a stealth thief. Learn to recognize and fight it successfully, and you may feel happier and healthier emotionally.)

It is absurd to make acting dependent on being distracted first. However, millions do it every day. Here's how this procrastination paradox works:

1. Tell a friend: "At some point, I will break my habit of hesitation."

2. Your friend suggests, "Why not start right away?"

3. Answer: "Yes. It sounds like a good idea. But I have to study procrastination, so I know what to do."

4. After collecting the materials to slip on, put them in a box. They say, "Now is not the right time. I have too much to do".

If you are sealed in the corner of your mind, such procrastination nonsense seems reasonable. If illuminated, these excuses reflect the logic of Swiss cheese. They are full of holes. So how can you find these conditional procrastination creations and then remove them from your mind?

The procrastination conditions are like a red herring mistake that takes you on a road where an emotional crisis is heading towards you. When you are tired of repeating these crises, look for spoiled red herring in your conditional thinking and throw them away by force. Here are three examples that illustrate this thinking:

1. You may hear an inner voice that forces you to linger. "You have to keep up with the tweets, so you don't lose your friends or lose important information. Tweet first. Work later." In your most thoughtful moments, see conditions as fictitious.

2. You can include yourself in a double agenda dilemma: end the priority or do something that takes away the priority activity. Here is a version of this wheedler with: "Now I deserve pleasure. If I satisfy my needs, I will end up with ___________." (They indicate the priority.)

3. Wait until you feel good before doing something that you and most others find uncomfortable. With this ease and convenience, you are prepared to procrastinate.

Three exercises to combat conditions

You can quickly learn to recognize conditional thinking that leads to delays. However, it is an informed effort to stop distracting you from these mental distractions.

When you see your conditions, (1) use them as red flags to indicate the impending procrastination risks. Pay attention to the signal, and you can quickly get back on the right track. (2) Use the condition as a reward for performing a priority action. With this loose-leaf technique, you can do something rewarding, like a cup of coffee after spending an hour preparing a presentation.

To support the concept of informed efforts, use the following properties, color wheel and priority techniques to combat and correct conditional thinking and stay productive:

Propinquity technology: propinquity means spatial and temporal closeness. A problem of propinquity arises when you are close to a situation that can trigger thoughts and feelings of anguish, e.g., For example if you have a business that you have not yet started and you are running out of time. Let's take a look at how deferral conditions affect a propinquity problem where you are late in cleaning.

Your apartment swells, and you feel stressed about the mess. You want to avoid the cleaning effort. They think "this is too much work." You decide to create a task list for the objects you want to delete. You have deleted the list. Your problem of propinquity continues.

You can avoid delay problems and avoid the penalties that usually follow. Start with a carryover analysis (replace the cleaning example with your proportionality problem). Use the results to refine your perspective on this topic and possibly change course.

1. What is the worst thing that can happen if I have to live with this situation for the next five years? What are the emotional costs?

2. What is the best thing that can happen if I have cleaned my house and prevented another mess in the next five years? What are the emotional costs?

3. What is the most likely result if I clean the mess and keep cleaning the house for the next five years? What are the emotional costs?

Are the costs of solving this problem lower or higher than those who live in chaos?

Color wheel technique: The color wheel game shows how to avoid distractions by drawing your attention to timely and effective actions.

Print an image of a color wheel on paper with a text cover. Write your highest priority on the hard drive where you see the green color, e.g., B. clean the house or prepare a speech. Write a word describing a condition for each of the other color segments, e.g., B. Waiting for the right mood.

Place the color wheel on a thin wooden stick (maybe a straw). Do it so that you can turn it like a pinwheel. Place a green marker on the pole. Spin the wheel: the part below the green dot indicates what you will do.

The chances are against the priority landing on the green dot. Now change the game where you can check the result. Instead of relying on luck, move the wheel to center the "green" priority under the green dot. Then start what you see.

Priority-based technology: the conditions are not all fictitious. Here is a production condition to break a deferral cycle: Overcoming the deferral is a by-product of something else is done first.

Implement the production conditions by doing the important thing without delay. In short, prevent deferral by setting your priorities. As a by-product, a pressure shift is prevented. You get even more, which is the biggest benefit.